GIFTS OF PRIDE AND LOVE:
KIOWA AND COMANCHE CRADLES

Barbara A Hail

Gifts of Pride and Love
KIOWA AND COMANCHE CRADLES

Edited by BARBARA A. HAIL

Introduction by N. SCOTT MOMADAY

Contributing Authors
JACOB AHTONE
JIMMY ARTERBERRY
RAY DOYAH
BARBARA A. HAIL
SHARRON AHTONE HARJO
VANESSA PAUKEIGOPE JENNINGS
JUANITA PAHDOPONY-MITHLO
BERNADINE HERWONA TOYEBO RHOADES
EVERETT R. RHOADES
CHRISTINA HUNT SIMMONS
BEATRICE AHPEAHTONE DOYAH SMITH
WECKEAH

HAFFENREFFER MUSEUM OF ANTHROPOLOGY

BROWN UNIVERSITY

HAFFENREFFER MUSEUM OF ANTHROPOLOGY
BROWN UNIVERSITY

STUDIES IN ANTHROPOLOGY
AND MATERIAL CULTURE, VOLUME VII

EXHIBIT SCHEDULE
GIFTS OF PRIDE AND LOVE
KIOWA AND COMANCHE CRADLES

December 1999 – March 2000
Gilcrease Museum, Tulsa, OK

April 2000 – July 2000
Heard Museum, Phoenix, AZ

August 2000 – January 2001
Fowler Museum of Cultural History, UCLA, Los Angeles, CA

March 2001 – May 2001
National Museum of the American Indian,
Gustav Heye Center, NYC

June 2001 – September 2001
Oklahoma Museum of Natural History, Norman, OK

October 2001 – January 2002
Mashantucket Pequot Museum and Research Center,
Ledyard, CT

FRONT COVER: A studio portrait of Autahntay (seated right), a relative of Hoygyohodle and the Rowell family, and other Mount Scott Kiowas, with baby in cradle made by Hoygyohodle. Photograph taken before 1904. The cradle is now in the Haffenreffer Museum of Anthropology, Brown University. Courtesy Western History Collections, University of Oklahoma Library, Phillips 826.

BACK COVER: Lattice cradle, Kiowa, c. 1880, made by Hoygyohodle (b. 1854). L: 119 cm. Walnut or bois-d'arc, native tanned deerskin, rawhide, glass seed beads, brass tacks, German silver studs, French brass beads, canvas, plain weave cotton, wool. Beads sinew-sewn directly on hide in old style. The cradle was made for a relative's baby; later, in 1904, it was given to her relative by marriage, George P. Rowell. Rudolf Haffenreffer purchased it in 1934. Haffenreffer Museum of Anthropology, Brown University, Rowell Collection 75-158. Photograph by Cathy Carver.

FRONTISPIECE: Lois Smoky (Kiowa) in cradle, 1904. Lois Smoky's mother and grandmother, Maggie Smoky and Makonte (Roman Nose), were excellent craftswomen known for their beadwork. Either one of them may have made this cradle. Lois grew up to become a well-known artist, often linked with the "Kiowa Five" as a "sixth" artist. The cradle is in the Museum of the Great Plains, Lawton, Oklahoma (see page 126). Photograph courtesy University of Pennsylvania Museum of Archaeology and Anthropology 54-141794.

Library of Congress Card Number: 00-101157
ISBN 0-912089-10-5

Distributed by Haffenreffer Museum of Anthropology, Brown University, Mount Hope Grant, Bristol, Rhode Island 02809
TEL: 401 253-8388   FAX: 401 253-1198

Funded by National Endowment for the Humanities, Haffenreffer Family Fund, National Endowment for the Arts, Haffenreffer Museum of Anthropology, Brown University

Produced by the Haffenreffer Museum of Anthropology,
Brown University and members of Kiowa and Comanche
cradle-making families

Kiowa and Comanche Consulting Committee

Jacob Ahtone, *Kiowa*
Jimmy Arterberry, *Comanche*
Weckeah Bradley, *Comanche*
Ray Doyah, *Kiowa*
Sharron Ahtone Harjo, *Kiowa*
Vanessa Paukeigope Jennings, *Kiowa/Kiowa*
  Apache/Pima
N. Scott Momaday, *Kiowa*
Juanita Pahdopony-Mithlo, *Comanche*
Linda Poolaw, *Kiowa/Delaware*
Bernadine Herwona Toyebo Rhoades, *Kiowa*
Everett R. Rhoades, *Kiowa*
Christina Hunt Simmons, *Kiowa*
Beatrice Ahpeahtone Doyah Smith, *Kiowa*

Other Project Members

Barbara A. Hail, *Project Director and Curator*
Stuart Parnes, *Exhibition Designer*
Rip Gerry, *Assistant Project Director*
Jacob Ahtone and Juanita Pahdopony-Mithlo,
  On-Site Coordinators
Alexandra O'Donnell, *Conservator*
Richard Ranlet, *Conservation Engineering*
Candace Greene, *Anthropological Consultant*
Lewis Lipsitt, *Consultant, Developmental Psychology*
Rip Gerry, Jamie Verinis, Kitto Weikert,
  DVant Digital, *Video Production*
Carolyn Udvardy, *Education Materials*
Thierry Gentis, *Registrar*

Dedicated to the Kiowa and Comanche people.

Cradles made by grandmothers and mothers, aunts and other relatives and passed down through generations were gifts of pride and love. Cradles collected by outsiders "got away" from the families that remembered the makers and recognized their skills. They became anonymous. At the heart of this book are Kiowa and Comanche cradles whose makers and family associations are known to us. From them we can imagine similar family connections for the larger body of cradles remaining un-named in collections around the world.

Table of Contents

"As We Saw Them at the Comanche Co. Fair." Cradle is in
Oklahoma Historical Society 78.101.1. Courtesy Sam DeVenney
Collection 1.

Foreword

IT IS AN HONOR to write a foreword for a project as skilled in design and execution, and pregnant with meaning, as *Gifts of Pride and Love: Kiowa and Comanche Cradles.* This catalogue, and the exhibition and video it accompanies, are products of an intensive collaboration between native people and a museum: between the descendants and relatives of makers of cradles placed in the Museum's care decades ago, on the one hand, and Barbara Hail and other members of the Haffenreffer Museum of Anthropology's staff on the other. That collaboration unfolded over years. In the early 1980s, these luminous and enchanting objects, which resonate in so many important ways for Kiowa and Comanche, caught Barbara Hail's curatorial eye and the Kiowa artist Sharron Ahtone Harjo's attention, and thus began the journey that, for the time being, culminates here.

It is always nice to hear from others that they appreciate the work of an institution to which one has dedicated one's time and energies. And so when Barbara Hail was unable to attend a meeting of principal investigators at National Endowment for the Humanities, and I went in her place, I heard from Endowment program administrators how much they admired this project and how it fit their idea of the ideal collaborative project between Indian country and museums.

Gifts of Pride and Love is the seventh number in the Haffenreffer Museum of Anthropology, Brown University series, *Studies in Anthropology and Material Culture.* Six other major catalogues have appeared in this series since 1975; the last number was *Passionate Hobby: Rudolf F. Haffenreffer and the King Philip Museum.* All have appeared in conjunction with major exhibitions at the Haffenreffer Museum. *Gifts of Pride and Love* – the exhibition – will travel nationally over a two-year period,

beginning at the Gilcrease Museum in December 1999, then proceeding to the Heard Museum, the Fowler Museum of Cultural History, the National Museum of the American Indian, and the Oklahoma Museum of Natural History, before ending at the final venue, the Mashantucket Pequot Museum and Research Center.

Gifts of Pride and Love continues the Haffenreffer Museum's strong interest in conveying to the public insights about the material culture and the lives of the people of the world. The people are often indigenous and the insights often derived from anthropology, which privileges understandings of the makers of objects and their descendants. The exhibition and catalogue and video also reflect our great concern over treating objects in the Museum's care with respect for the traditions of their makers.

In her acknowledgements, Barbara Hail thanks both institutions and people for their support. Here I would like to offer our sincere thanks just simply to the Kiowa and Comanche Consulting Committee, the National Endowment for the Humanities, National Endowment for the Arts, and Haffenreffer Family Fund. All provided fundamental support. All were indispensable. We are humbled by their trust in us. And we reciprocate with *Gifts of Pride and Love:* this catalogue, the exhibition, and the video.

SHEPARD KRECH III
Professor of Anthropology and
Director, Haffenreffer Museum of Anthropology

They are a safe haven for our children.

—SHARRON AHTONE HARJO

Back in those days infant mortality was high.
There were a lot of children born but not too many of them survived.
Very few of us own a cradleboard from the past;
it's a sort of reverence we have for them.
Its like cradleboards were a house for the beginning of life.

—LINDA POOLAW

We look at this cradle as representing a particular family;
we see that someone took time to create it;
we feel the love that it expresses; it speaks to us;
it tells us of our past.

—PHILIP BREAD

Always before making a cradle…
there were prayers for thanks, for the new baby
and for the material and for its gathering and use.
I continue in this road as I was shown
and feel that those who taught me are with me.
It gives a pleasant balance to my life.

—WECKEAH

They connect us to our past.

—BERNADINE HERWONA TOYEBO RHOADES

A Comanche mother and children, photographed by United
States census taker Julian Scott in Oklahoma Territory, 1890.
Courtesy University of Pennsylvania Museum of Archaeology
and Anthropology s4-141791.

Introduction

by N. SCOTT MOMADAY

THERE IS A VIVID IMAGE in my mind's eye. Two women sit in wooden chairs, one on either side of a window. The window frames a winter scene outside. The arbor stands away, vacant now, dark and cold within. The plain beyond slopes down to the Washita River. The red earth is visible beneath long tufts of dry grasses that waver in the cold wind. The sky is curdled, the color of pewter, and blurred. There are random flakes of snow swirling. But inside it is warm and cheerful. The sounds are of voices, low and congenial, and of a fire crackling in an iron stove. The two women are Kiowa matrons, in traditional dresses with wide sleeves and aprons. They wear their long hair in tight braids. Their eyes are very bright and their countenances serene. Their hands are remarkably expressive; they work deftly with needle and thread. One of these women is my grandmother, Aho. The other is Saintohoodle, a Kiowa captive who is my grandmother's close friend and neighbor. They bead and visit, visit and bead. It is a familiar activity, full of purpose and good feelings.

My Kiowa grandmother, Aho, was a beadworker of extraordinary skill. In *The Way to Rainy Mountain*, I wrote about the beautiful moccasins that she made for herself and that are now among my most cherished possessions.

> Aho's high moccasins are made of softest, cream-colored skins. On each instep there is a bright disc of beadwork – an eight-pointed star, red and pale blue on a white field – and there are bands of beadwork at the soles and ankles. The flaps of the leggings are wide and richly ornamented with blue and red and green and white and lavender beads.

She beaded well into her old age, making intricate and precise designs with her needle, without benefit of spectacles or artificial light. As a child I watched her work with fascination. She sat at a north window and sang lowly to herself. It was clear to me even then that her whole being was invested in her work. I use the word "work" for want of a better term. She did not think of what she was doing as work. Rather it was the creative expression of her spirit, like prayer, an expression that came from the center of her being. And that expression emanates from an ancient and spiritual source, I believe, and it persists in the blood. One of her great grandsons, Richard Aitson, is a renowned beadworker, and among his prized works are miniature cradleboards.

My grandfather, Mammedaty, built the house in which he and my grandmother lived and raised a family. It is where my father was born, and it was my first home. It still stands on a hill east of the town of Mountain View, above Rainy Mountain Creek. It is a ghost now, venerable and refined. Directly across the road is the house in which Saintohoodle, also known as Millie Durgan, lived. An historical marker on the roadside records that Millie Durgan was a white woman, captured as a child by the Kiowas in Texas in 1864. She married a Kiowa man, Goombi, and died in 1934, the year in which I was born. She was a cradleboard maker.

Kiowa and Comanche cradleboards are unique examples of Plains Indian iconography. Like shields, hide paintings, rawhide cases, and tipis, they are unmistakable components of material Plains culture. And certainly they are among the most intricately crafted of all such manufacture. And like these objects, too, the cradleboards remark the definitive mobility of the Plains people; they validate an ancient nomadism. And yet they are among the most recent manifestations

Mabel Hummingbird (Maunkaugoodle), Kiowa, born in 1886, was the daughter of Chief Hummingbird. Her mother, Quodledome'ty, made the toy cradle. Toy cradles were often exact miniatures of full-sized ones. Children learned the proper construction and use of cradles from playing with their toys. Mabel grew up to become a skilled beadworker, who made buckskin dresses for her grandchildren. Russell Studio, Anadarko, Oklahoma. Courtesy Sam DeVenney Collection 1-13.

of the culture. The earliest known cradles of this unique construction date from the middle of the nineteenth century. We might wonder why they appeared at that time. There is a bittersweet story in this, I believe.

In the middle of the nineteenth century the Plains Indian culture was in irreversible decline. Within a very short time, the Indians of the Great Plains suffered the loss of their land, their economy, and their religion with the encroachment of white settlement, the killing of the buffalo, and the prohibition of the Sun and Ghost dances. It was a time of nearly inconceivable desperation and despair.

The Kiowas and Comanches had always loved their children above all else. From the dim beginnings, it was understood that their way of life, predicated upon migration, hunting, and a warrior ideal, was always in the keeping of their children, one generation at a time. So long as their children came into the world, survival was a prospect, no matter how fragile it might be. The women began to make cradles, not so much for the sake of utility, but in thanksgiving and hope for the children, that they might live full lives and carry the blood of their ancestry beyond the moment in which extinction seemed most imminent. They made the cradles with profound love and faith, and they placed in them the whole strength and beauty of their spirit.

When you look closely at such a thing, you behold the sacred, and you come away with the gift of a great blessing.

A Comanche woman and her great-granddaughter, Anadarko, Oklahoma, 1900. Ties between generations were close in reservation times, since extended families settled close to one another, reflecting earlier family and band groupings. Grandparents played an important role in the lives of their grandchildren. Courtesy Western History Collections, University of Oklahoma Library, Phillips 674.

Fig. 1.1
Early Kiowa camp scene, with cradle and tipi. The women are
the wife (right) of Teehi and her mother. Courtesy Smithsonian
Institution 56387.

CHAPTER I

A House for the Beginning of Life

by BARBARA A. HAIL

Very few of us own a cradleboard from the past; it's a sort of reverence we have for them. It's like cradleboards were a house for the beginning of life.[1] —LINDA POOLAW, KIOWA-DELAWARE

WITH SUCH WORDS, Kiowa and Comanche people express their deep connection to their traditional cradles. In the late nineteenth century their ancestors created a unique art form that was both beautiful and functional. Great-grandmothers, grandmothers, mothers, and aunts, working together with male relatives, made the new lattice style cradle. Exquisitely beaded and lovingly prepared to receive an infant, it served as a "house for the beginning of life." For Kiowa and Comanche people a century ago, survival on the Oklahoma plains was far from easy. By making and exchanging these "gifts of pride and love," as one descendant of a cradle maker called them, family members and friends reflected close networks, which remained intact despite the difficult transition to reservation life, new religions, government boarding schools, and allotment of tribal lands.

This book is about these cradles and their makers. While a few remained in families, many of them "got away." Given or sold by Kiowas and Comanches, bought by both native and non-native people, cradles found their way into museums and private collections, where most became anonymous.

One such museum was the King Philip Museum in Bristol, Rhode Island. In 1934 Rudolf Haffenreffer, the museum's founder, purchased a collection made in the early years of this century by the Rowell family of Mount Scott, Oklahoma and Stamford, Connecticut.[2] Not only did the collection contain three Kiowa cra-

dles, but the names of their makers – Hoygyohodle, Daisy Mattonsaw, and Tahote – were recorded, which is unusual. After Rudolf Haffenreffer's death, his museum became, in 1955, the Haffenreffer Museum of Anthropology of Brown University. While Sharron Ahtone Harjo was a guest artist at the museum in 1981, she was stunned to discover a family connection. "The Rowells are my cousins," the Kiowa artist told me, "and I don't believe they know their cradles are here. I'll tell them when I go home." Eventually, Rowell family members came to see the cradles. Observing their intense delight in rediscovering familiar objects that had disappeared so long ago, I became determined to learn more about the gifted people who created them, and why they had lavished so much time and attention on them. Thus began a collaboration between descendants of cradle makers and the Haffenreffer Museum of Anthropology.

In 1995, when I first went to Oklahoma seeking information about early cradles, their makers, meanings, and history, Sharron Ahtone Harjo introduced me to her father. In turn, Jacob Ahtone introduced me to knowledgeable elders in his large, extended family and to friends in both Kiowa and Comanche communities. Juanita Pahdopony-Mithlo continued opening doors for me among the Comanche. Kiowa and Comanche people have played major roles in shaping the resulting research project, of which this book is one component. Cradle making has recently been revived, and artists working in beadwork and other media have become

Fig. 1.2
A Comanche family, at 2nd and C Avenue, Lawton, Oklahoma. With the cradle strapped around her shoulders, the woman's arms are free so that she can mount the wagon. Note the flowered cloth that can be pulled over the baby's face as a sun shield, and the leather *si'wuparru* or urine shield for this boy baby. Courtesy Museum of the Great Plains, Clifford Collection 3.

involved. Many elders, some in their eighties, contributed their knowledge. Forty Kiowa and twenty-five Comanche people participated in audio- and/or video-taped interviews. The thirteen descendants of cradle makers and present-day cradle-making artists who formed a Kiowa and Comanche Consulting Committee have been instrumental in the research, project design, exhibition, and publication. Committee members' memories of cradle makers in their families form the substance of this book, and tell us how much cradles mean to Kiowas and Comanches today.

LINKING CRADLES AND THEIR MAKERS

Each cradle is unique. Over four years, I compiled a data base with information on 180 cradles which, although far from exhaustive, is the largest assembled to date. Only two cradles were beaded with exactly the same designs; even then, one is a toy cradle, the other, full-size.[3] Did the same person make both cradles? If two people made them, were they related? The answer remains unknown.

One purpose of this project has been to identify the people who made cradles and to connect them with cradles in families and in public and private collections. Lattice cradle making is known as a woman's art. Women created the beaded covers; Kiowa and Comanche people call them the makers. Men often made the frames, but this contribution is considered less significant. Today only a few Kiowa and Comanche families have cradles, which have been used and handed down for many years. Thirty-eight cradles are illustrated in this book; we know who made twenty-five of them, and we know the families to whom another seven belonged.

As I interviewed Kiowa people, it became apparent that, although the physical objects were gone, the memory of cradles endured. Many women could recite the names of six or seven excellent cradle makers of past generations in their own or other's families. They remembered what their family cradles looked like. They recalled the cherished cradles, made by their grandmothers or other female relatives, that hung in their home. "We had it for years and years on the wall all covered up so that it wouldn't get any dust," said one Kiowa elder.[4]

It became equally apparent that almost no one knew where their own family cradle was. Sadly, they had just "gotten away," people told me. In the early twentieth century, as cradles became recognized for their beauty, they had been snapped up by collectors and museums. In years of terrible hardship, a few dollars in cash seemed irresistible. As one elder phrased it: "My mother accepted $75 for her cradle, and was rich for a few days. But then the whole thing was gone forever."[5]

As I conducted research in U.S. museums and private collections, I located almost two hundred cradles.

Fig. 1.3
Kiowa cradle maker Doyetone *(Digging for Medicine)* (1853–1926) and her husband Honemeeda, the son of Tohauson, chief of the Kiowa for thirty-three years. Doyetone was a master beadworker whose name became a byword for excellence. "Who do you think you are – Doyetone?" was a familiar way of teasing aspiring beadworkers. Courtesy Dorothy White Horse DeLaune Collection.

The more I admired the beauty of the object, the more disappointed I became at how rarely the maker's name had accompanied it. For example, James Mooney, an anthropologist who worked extensively with the Kiowas at the turn of the century, collected six cradles for the National Museum of Natural History, Smithsonian Institution, and one for the Field Museum of Natural History, Chicago. Although he most likely knew the names of the women who made them, he did not record them. Perhaps the maker purposely withheld her name, seeing no reason for it to go with the object, which would never be seen again in her community. Through such omissions, cradle makers who are proudly remembered in their communities have largely become invisible outside them.

Correlating the cradles, museum and archival records, photographs, and memories became one of the most challenging and rewarding aspects of the project. Photographs were particularly useful in this regard. At the turn of the century, formal studio photographs of native American families often showed parents dressed in their finest and the infant in a cradle placed prominently in the foreground (see cover). Sometimes a cradle in a collection was also depicted in a historic photograph, and interviews with families who used that cradle yielded information about its maker (fig. 1.3, and see pages 122, 123). Examining both objects and photographs, people identified features such as beadwork designs, which led to discussions about the association between specific designs and makers, and whether designs were handed down in families.

While the lattice cradle is a commonly recognized symbol of the arrival of one new life, today it is even more important as a symbol of the continuity of all Kiowa and Comanche life. "We look at this cradle as representing a particular family; we see that someone took time to create it; we feel the love that it expresses; it speaks to us; it tells us of our past."[6] Thus Philip and Carrie Bread, a Kiowa and Comanche couple, acknowledged the cradles' power to give people vital information about their identity. Their children were fortunate enough to have been in a family cradle. Reminding people of their ancestors' long, arduous struggles to create and maintain a viable identity, cradles connect them with their past.

Kiowa and Comanche people are closely associated with the Southern Plains, but they were on the move for several centuries. The Kiowa lived among the Crows in present-day Montana in the seventeenth and eighteenth centuries, then moved gradually to the Black Hills, South Dakota, accompanied by the smaller Kiowa-Apache (Plains Apache) tribe.[7] They settled in their present Southern Plains location around 1820. The Comanche lived with their allies the Shoshones near the Rocky Mountain headwaters of the Arkansas River until the early 1700s. They migrated south to present-day New Mexico, then into Texas. While Kiowa and Comanche tribes initially clashed, competing for hunting territories, since the early nineteenth century they have been allies (fig. 1.4).

From the first half of the eighteenth century, when Spanish-introduced horses had become widely available as a means of successfully hunting buffalo, Kiowa, Comanche, and Kiowa-Apache tribes shared a life style with other high plains nomads, characterized by seasonal movements of camps that followed similar paths year after year within roughly defined hunting territories. Rivalry for these hunting territories and for possession of horses led to intermittent raiding, and a system of war honors based on individual bravery. Male prestige was dependent on success in warfare and amassing wealth through horses and portable trade goods. The Kiowa, a ranked society, accorded the most prestige to their *Koi tsa gah*, or "ten bravest men." Camps were loosely organized into bands, with chiefs chosen for leadership qualities. The people had a strong spiritual identification with the land and the natural forces within it. Gathering in early summer for annual Sun Dance ceremonies, they celebrated the continuing renewal of the life forces of the world, the tribe, and the individual, all tied inextricably to the one great source of their subsistence – the bison. There was clear division of labor. Men were responsible for providing food and for protecting the camp against enemies. Women

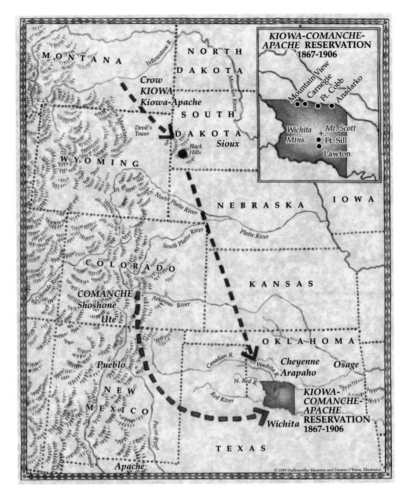

Fig. 1.4
Kiowa, Kiowa-Apache, and Comanche tribal migrations and reservation. Map by Dennis O'Brien.

were responsible for maintaining and moving the camps, nurturing the children, and preparing hide clothing, tipis, and household articles.

By the mid-nineteenth century, non-Indian settlers were moving steadily into the Southern Plains in search of land, resulting in conflicts with native people. In 1867 a treaty confederated the Kiowa with the Comanche and Kiowa-Apache and assigned them to live in a restricted area of southwestern Oklahoma. Their mobile lifestyle ended. At Fort Sill, a U.S. Army post was established in their midst, and a government agency administered Indian affairs and provided food and supplies (fig. 1.5). The rations proved insufficient, and their delivery unreliable.

Kiowa and Comanche hunting parties continued to ride out in search of buffalo, even as commercial hide hunters, with the complicity of the U.S. Army, decimated the buffalo herds. The Kiowa and Comanche also continued to raid for horses, an important source of wealth, in Texas and Mexico. The Kiowa, Comanche, Arapaho, Cheyenne, and Apache often joined forces in the 1860s–70s, battling to retain their hunting territories. Following a bitter conflict with the army in 1874 at Palo Duro Canyon, Texas, the people returned wearily to the reservation. Many of their leaders had been captured or killed. Giving up armed resistance, they were urged by the government to attempt a new way of life as farmers.

During the reservation period (1867–1906) the Kiowas' and Comanches' entire way of life changed. Men lost their traditional role as warriors who provided for and protected their people. Children were sent to government day and boarding schools, where they were forbidden to speak their own language. Their hair was cut short, and their traditional clothing taken away and replaced with school uniforms (fig. 1.6). In 1877, in an effort to further wean the people from the nomadic life-style represented by tipis, the government began building houses for them.[8]

The final Kiowa Sun Dance was held in 1887, after which people put away the ritual materials and vowed to end practice forever. Beginning about 1890, some Kiowas joined a messianic ghost dance religion, which promised that beloved ancestors and the buffalo would return and the white man and his hated cattle would

disappear. Others found comfort in combining Christian teachings with the peyote cult, forming the Native American Church. For most, Christian church missions became a focus for the new way of life.[9]

In 1892, against the Indian people's wishes, the government bowed to pressure from non-Indians for land and surveyed reservation lands. They took a census in preparation for allotment. Through this each tribal member would receive an individual homestead of 160 acres, with the remaining land sold to the United States government for eventual resale by lottery to non-Indians. As a result, almost two and a half million acres of the original 2,968,893 acres that had been assigned as reservation lands at the 1867 Medicine Lodge council moved out of Indian hands.[10] During reservation times Kiowas and Comanches had resided in close, multi-generational units, reflecting earlier family and band groupings, and members of extended families continued this pattern by selecting adjacent allotments. Between 1901 and 1903 individuals had to enroll at the agency, writing their name, age, and relationship as head of household, wife, or child, or they would be denied an allotment. According to the 1870 census, 5,938 individuals lived on the Kiowa-Comanche-Apache Reservation: 1,896 Kiowas, 300 Kiowa-Apaches, and 3,742 Comanches. Only about half of this number had registered and received allotments by 1906 when the reservation was finally terminated.[11] The end of the reser-

Fig. 1.5
Drawing rations at Fort Sill Sub Agency. The woman on the left is about to wrap a blanket around the child on her back. Courtesy Museum of the Great Plains, Arthur Lawrence Collection 1077.

Fig. 1.6
Fort Sill School children seated on grass. Courtesy Museum of the Great Plains, Arthur Lawrence Collection 1028.

vation also brought the end of government food rations and the beginning of really hard times. Confined to a small amount of land, in order to survive, the people had to farm or find other ways to use their lands.

Despite these drastic upheavals, the reservation and immediate post-reservation period proved ones of expansion in artistic output. Women, no longer occupied with continual packing and movement of camps, had more time in their new sedentary environment to devote intense creative energy into decorating clothing and other articles. In the mid 1880s Comanches, in particular, began to lease their land to non-Indian Texas cattle ranchers, and the "grass" payments provided a semi-annual flow of cash into the reservation. This attracted licensed traders, who built permanent trading posts and provided heretofore scarce items – cloth, glass beads, finished lumber, and household goods such as linoleum.[12] Perhaps searching for ways to reinforce tribal identity and family unity in a period of cultural loss, women utilized these new materials to create beautifully decorated cradleboards. Particularly among the Kiowa, the broad surface of the sides of the cradle cover inspired a multitude of brilliant color and design combinations. These became prestige objects, given in pride and love to special infants. At the same time, they were a short-lived extravagance, since times were changing quickly. By the early 1900s, as reservation lands opened to non-Indians, town grew up almost overnight, and non-Indian settlement brought new goods that Indian women quickly coveted. In childcare,

this included such things as high chairs, cribs, and baby carriages. As early as 1891 the anthropologist James Mooney observed: "These Indians are now receiving their money from the lands recently sold, and are consequently reveling in store goods....You see more baby carriages now than Indian cradles. In a few months this country will be opened and then goodby to Indian life (fig. 1.7)."[13] All these factors would influence and transform, but not eliminate, an object that was once a vital part of traditional camp life – the portable cradle.

Fig. 1.7
Martha Napawat's baby Thomas in a carriage, Anadarko, Oklahoma, 1901. Martha, a Kiowa, was married to a Comanche. She was educated at the Carlisle Indian School. Courtesy Western History Collections, University of Oklahoma Library, Phillips 206.

Comanche cradles are packed on horseback on long journeys and the way they are carried is strange indeed. The Comanches take a plank, a little longer and a little wider than the infant, and build sides onto it so as to form a sort of lidless case. This they line with soft skins and place the baby upon them, holding him securely in the cradle by means of straps wrapped around it. Usually the top plank projects a little beyond the infant's head, so that a line can be passed through a hole bored for the purpose. When a *rancheria* is on the march you may see the women on horseback with their babies swinging from the pommels of their saddles, for all the world like so many pistols. When they reach the day's campsite the mothers may swing the cradles from the branch of a tree, or prop them against a convenient rock, and so they nurse their babies.[14]

Thus Jean Louis Berlandier, a French biologist, described cradles as used in western Texas in 1828. Kiowa and Comanche people with whom I have consulted agree that long ago, cradles were carried on horseback, hanging from saddle pommels. Berlandier provides evidence that cradles were used this way, although he described a "lidless case" rather than a lattice cradle. It was probably a type of board cradle, which was used across North America, including some parts of the Southern Plains, in the early 1800s. This type is made of a solid board backing, to which the infant is secured with wrappings.

Berlandier's description stands out in the sparse written and pictorial record of Southern Plains cradles before the 1860s. The artist Samuel Seymour accompanied a government-sponsored scientific expedition led by Major Stephen H. Long to explore the Great Plains in 1820–21. In "A Kiowa Encampment," Seymour sketched mothers holding babies in their laps, but no cradles.[15] George Catlin, who sketched Kiowa and Comanche camps in movement in 1833–34, portrayed women and children riding double and triple on horseback, but no cradles.[16] Twenty years later, Friedrich Richard Petri, a German immigrant, painted a watercolor of a Plains mother on mule-back in Texas, balancing a very young child in front of her – still no cradle.[17]

In the late 1860s the lattice cradle began to appear in both collections and documentation. The lattice cradle is known as *paih'dodl* (wrap handle) in Kiowa and *waakohno* (cedar carrier) in Comanche.[18] Commonly termed a cradleboard, it was the preferred type among the Kiowa and Comanche from about 1870 to 1920. Arapaho, Cheyenne, and Lakota people also adopted and modified the type, using it along with other types.

The lattice cradle consisted of a cover, made of hide (later, canvas and wool), wrapped around rawhide supports at the head and foot, with a rawhide backing. This whole assemblage was laced to a frame, composed of two narrow pointed boards and two shorter, narrower cross pieces, which formed a modified V-shaped lattice construction. The sturdy construction protected the infant, with a rawhide hood around its face and strong boards and rawhide at its back (see fig. 1.12). The V-shape provided an opening for the mother's head while she carried the cradle, and when she leaned it against a tree or post, with one board on either side, prevented it from slipping (see figs. 1.20, 11.7).

The earliest illustration of a lattice cradle I have seen appears in an 1867 *Harper's Weekly* (fig. 1.8). Theodore R. Davis's drawing shows a woman, probably Kiowa or Kiowa Apache, wearing a lattice-style cradle on her back, at a trading post in Fort Dodge, Kansas. Operated by John Tappan and William S. Soule, the store did a

Fig. 1.8
Sketch of a lattice cradle worn by a woman, probably Kiowa or Kiowa-Apache, in a sutler's store in Fort Dodge, Kansas in 1867, by Theodore R. Davis. Courtesy *Harper's Weekly* 6(543):329, May 25, 1867.

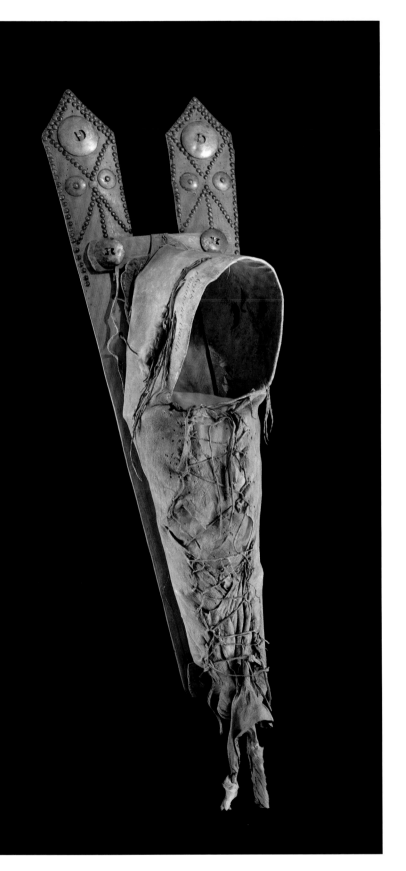

thriving business with the military, squatters, civilian employees, and Indians. Their Indian customers were mostly Kiowa and Kiowa Apache, since the Cheyenne and Arapaho in the area were hostile at the time.[19]

The next year (1868) Edward Palmer, a botanist, collected two cradles at the same time from the Comanche in Texas. Both are now in the Smithsonian's National Museum of Natural History. One was a *waakohno*, cedar carrier or lattice style cradle. The earliest waakohno known to me, it is illustrated in the *National Museum Report for 1887* (fig. 1.9).[20] The other was a *haabikʉno*, tubular cradle, of curved raw animal hide with the hair side turned inward to create a soft bed for the infant (fig. 1.10).[21] The haabikʉno, also called a "lying down cradle" or "night cradle," predated the waakohno among the Comanche and continued after it, through the mid-twentieth century.

The origin of the lattice style is unknown. It resembles both the haabikʉno and the Navajo split board cradle. It may have developed by attaching two wood slats to a rawhide haabikʉno, enabling a woman to carry a child on her back, freeing her hands. It may be a variant of the Navajo cradle, which has a split-cedar board back and soft wrappings and ties in front, but Navajo board extensions are short with the tips rounded or straight, there is a curved wooden bow over the baby's face, and the split boards are laced together with no lattice framework and no rawhide supports.[22]

The lack of pictorial evidence of the lattice cradle before the late 1860s, its limited distribution, and the simultaneous use of other types of cradles by the Comanches and other nearby tribes indicate that it may have originated as recently as 1860. Twentieth-century artists often depicted cradles on horses: women carry them in their arms or on their back; cradles hang from

Fig. 1.9
Early lattice cradle, Comanche, called *waakohno* (cedar carrier) collected by Edward Palmer in 1868. L: 106.5 cm. Osage orange (bois d'arc) boards with large German silver hair plates and smaller bosses laced on; unbeaded, tanned deerskin cover with deer hair remaining on tabs at bottom; buffalo rawhide back; twisted fringe of buffalo hide and hair around head; red wool carrying strap with harness leather buckle. Department of Anthropology, Smithsonian Institution 6918. Photograph by Cathy Carver.

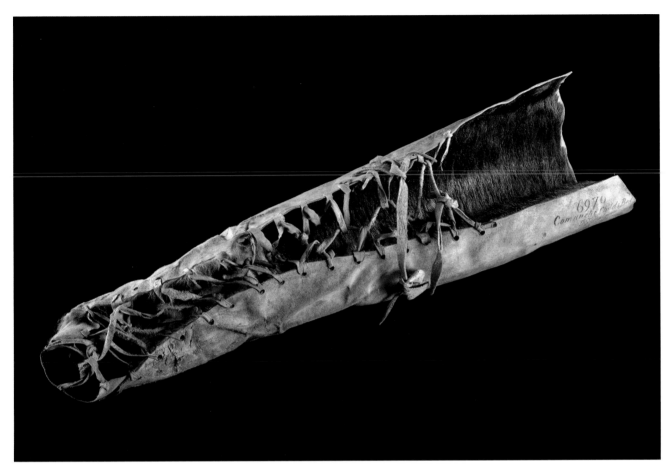

Fig. 1.10
Early rawhide cradle, Comanche, called *haabikᵻno* (lying down or night cradle), collected by Edward Palmer in 1868. L: 80 cm. Rolled rawhide tube, hair (black and white) side in, front lacing, with separate rounded footrest attached with thong laces. Department of Anthropology, Smithsonian Institution 6970. Photograph by Cathy Carver.

the saddle pommel or rest on a travois.[23] At the turn of the century, women using lattice cradles on horseback are depicted in a few photographs (fig. 1.11, and see page 125). Yet the earliest lattice cradle with firm documentation was collected in 1868, by which date most Kiowa and Comanche people were already settled on reservation lands and extensive movements on horseback of entire camps were no longer part of daily life. Although the lattice cradle is associated with horseback use and a nomadic lifestyle, its most elaborate, ornately beaded form blossomed during a period of cultural transition, as settled reservation life replaced mobile camp life.

Fig. 1.11
A young Kiowa girl has hung her doll cradle from her saddle pommel. Fourth of July parade, Anadarko, Oklahoma, 1894. Courtesy Western History Collections, University of Oklahoma Library, Phillips 498.

For about fifty years, from 1870–1920, both Kiowa and Comanche people produced lattice cradles. In their heyday, many of these cradles were extravagantly decorated with glass beads. Several other styles of lattice cradle were made simultaneously by Central Plains tribes, and the designs and materials also changed over time. Systematic comparison of many examples has been facilitated by the database I have compiled.

Kiowa and Comanche Cradles Compared
Kiowa cradles and Comanche cradles have distinctive features which make it possible to distinguish one group's work from the other's, but only to a certain extent. The cradle collected from the Comanche in 1868 (see fig. 1.9) resembles those made in the 1870s–80s by both Comanche and Kiowa people. Later the two tribes differed in their decoration and attachments. Through the years, the Comanche have continued to prefer undecorated covers and elaborate boards, preferably of cedar, with tips decorated with incised, pigment-filled lines, pigment-covered surfaces, and metal studs, buttons, or tacks. One such pigment was a red mineral, *equipsia,* found in layers of clay in Jimmy Creek, near Mount Scott, according to cradle-maker Weckeah Bradley. A deep purple vegetable dye, made of a tiny forest berry, was also rubbed on boards.[24]

The size of Kiowa and Comanche cradles is remarkably consistent in total length, width, and depth. Comanche cradles are slightly wider. The average cradle measurements for the forty full-size Kiowa cradles I have measured are (without fringe): length 45″, width 13 1/5″, depth 10 10/10″. The Kiowa also made a slightly smaller cradle, called "newborn" size, about 39″ long.[25] The average measurements for the thirty Comanche cradles I have measured are: length 45″, width 13 2/5″, depth 10 9/10″. On both, the cover usually extends to about 1 1/2–2″ above the lower end of the boards, but may be higher or lower, sometimes reaching to the end of the boards.[26]

Kiowa cradles featured a bib. Made of hide or cloth, it was decorated with beads or sequins and attached just above the cradle cover, covering the joining of the upper cross-piece to the boards. Kiowas often added brass tacks or German silver buttons to the tops of the boards, but did not normally paint the boards. At the foot of the cover, the Comanche placed a rectangular wooden footrest, which protruded at a right angle. Kiowa covers had no footrest, and cover bottoms were usually rounded, and finished with hide fringes up to fifteen inches long. Sometimes, in place of fringe, Kiowa cradles featured hide tabs, often beaded, at the top and bottom of the front lacing. Sometimes the tabs were fringed.

By the last decade of the century, several notable changes occurred as trade materials replaced natural products. Cradle covers were originally made of hide, and the beads were attached with sinew. As Kiowa women began to fill the surface of their covers completely with bead embroidery, they also began to replace the hide with canvas, which they beaded using steel needles and thread, newly available from traders and easier to use than awl and sinew. A small strip of hide was sewn to the canvas on either side of the front lacing to hold the hide loops through which the thong lacing was threaded; a strip of hide was also often added around the head opening, and a fabric lining attached to it; and the hide tabs and fringes remained. Since the canvas body of the cover was completely beaded, the cradle still looked as if it were made entirely of hide. The back of the cradle was originally of rawhide. By

Fig. 1.12
Lattice cradle structure showing rawhide supports at head and foot and rawhide backing. A cover was wrapped around the rawhide. Model by Carl Jennings.

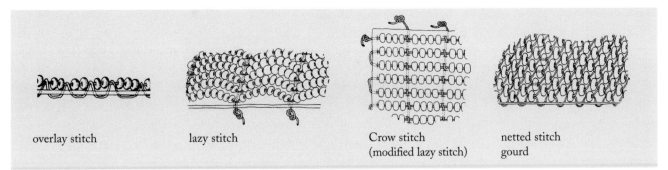

overlay stitch lazy stitch Crow stitch (modified lazy stitch) netted stitch gourd

Fig. 1.13
Chart of bead stitch types. Courtesy Haffenreffer Museum of Anthropology, Brown University.

1900 linoleum had replaced rawhide in a number of cradles. Linings were originally of soft tanned hides, and these were gradually replaced with available fabrics, from flour sacks to cotton prints to velvets. A sunshield made of a cotton cloth was frequently tied to the cover in the head area, and could be drawn over the child's face as needed.

Bead designs were bold in color, often outlined with multiple rows of different colors, the outer rows usually white, contrasting against a blue, green, or red background. Sometimes dark outlined designs appeared on a white background. Blue is the most commonly used background color. They used a combination of stitches (fig. 1.13). A curvilinear, abstract floral, leaf, or amorphous shape was normally executed in an overlay stitch with straight interior rows and raised outlining, and a Crow stitch background. Geometric designs were normally executed in lazy stitch, as was their background, without raised outlining.[27] Both Kiowa and Comanche women used the netted stitch on some cradles (see pages 118, 125 and fig. 7.4). Only one cradle I have examined employs all of these stitches (see fig. 2.1).

The design layout of the cover has several basic formats. The Kiowa cover's sides were often asymmetrical in color, design, or both.[28] In one typical layout, Kiowa beadworkers divided the design field of the cover into three units. The two lower units were usually alike. The top unit was different and sometimes spanned the entire head area. Another layout was essentially the same but at the top a line of beadwork divided the cover into two equal design fields. In a third layout, one side had abstract curvilinear designs and the other, geometric. A few fully beaded cradles have representational designs, including heraldic emblems, houses, tipis, and horses and riders.[29]

Early in the twentieth century, red wool became a popular material for Kiowa covers. These covers were not fully beaded; rather, the designs were widely spaced on the surface to reveal a considerable amount of red background (see page 124).

Although the Comanches typically used undecorated hide covers, they did bead the covers of special cradles, called *tʉrokohno*, or *tsomo waakohno*. Some fully beaded Comanche cradles used patterns found on other Comanche objects, such as dress tabs and peyote equipment, often in netted or flat gourd stitch. Designs were usually geometric, made up of small elements, predominantly in white, blue, and red. The netted stitch lends itself to small geometric designs. Mary Buffalo, a Kiowa woman, was photographed on horseback about 1916 carrying this type of Comanche net-beaded cradle (see page 125). Her first husband was Comanche, and this cradle may have been a gift from her husband's family for her first son, Homer.[30]

Around the head opening, people hung long strands of necklace beads, seeds, small gourds, metal filigree, and other objects which could dangle in front of the baby's face, serving as portable toys. Comanche cradles tend to have more of these appendages.

Cradles included certain hygienic features. In 1935 Mary Buffalo recalled the earlier Kiowa practice of placing a hide flap filled with buffalo hair or some other material in the cradle, to serve as a diaper, and removing it when soiled, by undoing just the lower section of the front lacings.[31] Comanche boy's cradles included a unique feature called a shield, or *si'wʉparrʉ* (fig. 1.14). A piece of commercial harness leather, cut, shaped, and sometimes beaded, was attached to the lower half of the cover with thongs. The infant's penis would be rested on this leather shield so he could urinate outside the cradle and not stain the interior.

Harness leather became a common material for cradles, awl cases, and other small bags, in part because it was readily available at Fort Sill, where many Apache, Kiowa, and Comanche men were employed in various capacities. After the close of the Indian Wars in the mid 1870s, a detachment of Indian Scouts served at Fort Sill; and in 1892, Troop L, Seventh Cavalry, was formed under the command of Lt. Hugh Scott, composed mostly of Kiowa soldiers.[32] A soldier's worn out horse tack or riding boots could be re-worked into carrying straps, bibs, and si'wᵾparrᵾ. Carrying straps made of harness leather sometimes retained the metal buckle.

Commercially prepared lumber was readily available by the turn of the century, as Fort Sill, Lawton, and Anadarko grew rapidly. Lumber from packing crates, discarded furniture, and abandoned wagons could be had at no cost and re-worked into boards for cradles.

Despite the numerous distinct stylistic and construction features, it is difficult to attribute every cradle definitively to either a Kiowa maker or a Comanche maker. The two groups lived adjacent to one another, shared a political and economic base on the Kiowa-Comanche-Apache reservation, and frequently intermarried. Cradles made by members of one tribe were often traded, sold, or given to the other. As they changed hands, cradles were modified. Footrests and si'wᵾparrᵾ were added and removed. The same beaded cover was used successively on different boards. Most often this was done after a Kiowa-made cradle moved into a Comanche family. Such changes are shown in many historic photographs. For example, a 1904 photograph shows Lois Smoky, a Kiowa baby, in a cradle with Kiowa-style tack decorated boards (frontispiece). Today the same cradle has Comanche-style painted boards, probably acquired when it later belonged to the Comanche Monetathchi family (see page 126). Even when they remained within one family, cradle covers were sometimes removed from the boards and put away for several years, until the birth of a new baby created a reason to bring them out. Then family members would re-attach the boards, or carve new ones, create a new

Fig. 1.14
Dorothea Tenequer Komacheet, Comanche (l), and her baby, Bertha, and an unidentified woman and infant boy. Comanche girls' cradles differed from those of the boys. Boys' cradles were equipped with a piece of harness leather called a *si'wᵾparrᵾ* laced to the lower half which deflected the baby's urine from the cradle. Courtesy Western History Collections, University of Oklahoma Library, SWOC 228.

bib, mend or replace linings and lacings, and use the cradle again.[33]

Designers and Designs
During the last third of the nineteenth century, Kiowa and Comanche clothing, except for small items, was not fully beaded, but was trimmed with narrow edgings in geometric line designs, fringes, metal cones, and pigments. Therefore, the decision to bead completely the broad surface of the cradle cover required a conscious break with the habitual manner of using beads. Designs were sometimes inspired by nearby tribes, and sometimes beadwork was even done by them.

Neighboring native people who moved into Oklahoma Territory from the east in the nineteenth century used curvilinear and abstract floral bead designs, especially the prairie and mid-Missouri River people such as the Oto, Missouri, and Mesquakie, and the Delaware and Shawnee, originally from further east.[34] Delaware bandolier bags and other objects commonly featured asymmetrical color and design, as Kiowa cradles and moccasins did later.

Many cradles are beaded in geometric designs. Apache women living at Fort Sill made beadwork with geometric designs in small units. Textiles with geometric designs woven by the Navajo, Hispanic and native communities in the Rio Grande area, and various groups in Mexico, particularly Saltillo serapes, may have influenced cradle design.[35] A major trade existed between the Kiowa and Comanche people and Hispanic traders coming from Taos and Santa Fe. It is also possible that Kiowa and Comanche raiding parties, who continued riding into Texas and Mexico until the mid-1870s after horses, captives, and other wealth, brought weavings home.

A number of cradles which are unmistakably Kiowa/Comanche in structure have been beaded in Cheyenne style designs.[36]

> My grandmother, Flora Niyah Roach, told me that, in the early 1900s, because our work was kind of plain and made for a purpose – of course we loved beautiful things too, but we just didn't put that much emphasis on doing it because life was really…too tough – and so we started asking the Cheyenne women to bead our cradles. Obviously we trusted them because the cradle's something very special and you're not just going to trust anybody. The Comanche would construct it and then ask the Cheyenne women to bead it.[37]

Jimmy Arterberry, a Comanche cradle maker, invoked his grandmother's words to explain the Comanches' taste for Cheyenne beadwork. Cheyenne women, immediate neighbors to the north, were excellent bead workers. Intermarriage also played a role in mixing design styles. The cradle maker Sahkolmah (Cheyenne Woman), great-great-great-grandmother of present-day cradle maker Richard Aitson, was from the Black Kettle band of Cheyenne and married a Kiowa man.

Colors used on some cradles, including pinks, light blue, yellow, and lavender or periwinkle, are reminiscent of late nineteenth-century Crow beadwork. The "Crow stitch," frequently used to bead the background on Kiowa cradles, is so called because the Crow used it on horse chest ornaments and on beaded tabs hanging from saddle pommels and cantles, and on other broad areas. Since the time Kiowa people lived in the Northern Plains, many maintained close ties and family relationships with Crow tribe members. Regular visits back and forth provided an opportunity for craftswomen to exchange ideas of color and stitch techniques.[38]

Some designs have specific meanings. One geometric pattern incised and painted on the upper ends of Comanche boards apparently represented origins: "who we are and where we came from; that is, the darkness symbolic of our People's entrance into this world."[39] On many cradles, both Kiowa and Comanche, a four-directional motif has been beaded on the cover on either side of the baby's head, probably as symbolic protection (see figs. 2.8, 5.1, 9.1).

Each woman created her own designs. Among the Kiowa, natural forms often inspired artists. "Every tribe has its own way of doing things. There is a Kiowa way of making designs, and there is a Comanche way," said Gina Quoetone Ware Paughty (1913–1996), an elder skilled in beadworking. She said one typical Kiowa trademark was the leaf, a widespread and highly varied design, which she called *aiyedaihkwoot,* "something like a leaf" or a "leaf picture."[40] It apparently depicts an oak leaf, probably the burr oak or post oak, formerly common in Oklahoma. Like several others, Paughty firmly stated that a leaf was never copied exactly or traced; each artist held the idea of the leaf in her mind and interpreted it differently. She might give or lend the design to others or keep it as her own individual mark. Copying designs without the original creator's consent was considered improper.

Multiple cradles by the same artist reveal her individual style. The designs on two cradles by Guohaddle or "Mesquite Beans" (1853–1933) are remarkably similar but not exactly alike (figs. 3.1, 3.4). Guohaddle created several variations of leaf-like designs, cutting them out of meat-packing paper and tracing in pencil around them. According to her granddaughter, "the designs were Grandmother's own, and no one else's, unless she gave permission for them to be used."[41]

The cradle primarily symbolizes birth and the addition of a new member to the tribe, and by extension stands for the importance of family life and the nurturing of children. More broadly, the cradle has come to symbolize Kiowa and Comanche social and cultural life in its entirety. Not only did actual cradles play important social roles in daily and ritual life, but images of them pervade other media.

In the late nineteenth century, Bad Eye, a Kiowa, made drawings of lattice cradles on five of 57 pages in a ledger book (fig. 1.15). In 1904, Silver Horn painted a calendar of the years 1828–1904. In it the Kiowa artist noted significant events for every year, including births and deaths. Births are indicated by small images of cradles, often connected to a name glyph. He used the lattice cradle glyph throughout, implying that the form already existed in the earlier years (fig. 1.16). Silver Horn not only lived during the heyday of cradle making, but was related to the cradle makers Keintaddle, Maud Rowell, Tahdo, Daisy Mattonsaw, and Paukeigope. For him, the lattice cradle was the most widely understood sign of the arrival of a new life, and thus an appropriate icon for his annual record of events.

The value of the cradle was far from exclusively symbolic. The object itself had value as a way to physically protect life, a means to create kinship and society, and a work of art. The social life of objects is always characterized by shifting insertions into different regimes of value that correspond to the cultural systems of the people who use them.[42] During the period of maximal cradle production and use, native and non-native people increasingly came into contact. As Kiowa and Comanche life has changed, so too has the way in which cradles are valued and used.

The Baby in the Cradle: Physical and Psychological Effects

> The cradleboard symbolizes a safe haven for an infant; the way it was wrapped up, the way it was carried, on the back, on the same level as the mother. If it's sitting down on the ground and the mom is sitting down it was on equal view with the mother. If carried on a horse, the same. It was placing the child in a position so it could see, on an adult level.[43]

Fig. 1.15
Page from a Ledger Book drawn by Bad Eye, Kiowa, collected ca. 1890. Courtesy Fairbanks Museum and Planetarium, St. Johnsbury, Vermont, cat. 7743.

Fig. 1.16
Page for winter 1868–69 from Annual Calendar covering the years 1828 through 1904, re-drawn by Silver Horn for anthropologist James Mooney in ink and watercolor wash on paper in 1904. Births are noted by small images of cradles connected to a name glyph. It was based on a calendar begun by Tohausen, who initiated calendar keeping among the Kiowa, and carried on by his nephew Agiati, and then by Agiati's son Silver Horn. The pencil notations of names, added by James Mooney, include: "1 son of Gual-hyu-I=Wild Horse Colt; Mainhodeti born; Settanti 1st arrested; Lone Wolf releast & returns; Da-I-bai born." Courtesy Candace Greene, National Museum of Natural History from Smithsonian Institution Ms. 2531, vol. 7, INV08894100.

Sharron Ahtone Harjo, descendant of two Kiowa cradle makers, emphasizes security and socialization as important aspects of cradle use. Like other Kiowa and Comanche women, she strongly believes that the upright position of the lattice cradle, worn on the mother's back, at eye level with adults, helped to socialize infants and to make them immediately sense they were a part of the tribal community. The stimulation of frequent eye and voice contact, which encourages development in infants, is facilitated by close proximity to the mother. The upright position is also one of the safest for an infant and may help prevent SIDS (Sudden Infant Death Syndrome).[44] Another type of cradle, the Comanche *haabikuno*, "night cradle," was specifically made for sleeping. Older Comanche women remembered it as a safe place for the swaddled *(nahdu)* baby, who could then lay in bed between sleeping adults without risk of being crushed.

Kiowa and Comanche women wrapped very young babies before placing them in the cradleboard, and reported only positive results (fig. 1.17). Interviews with elders elicited strong feelings about the beneficial and quieting effects of swaddling and the resultant immobility. Older women who recalled the custom of wrapping an infant with the arms tucked inside the blanket insisted that the baby quieted down when so secured, whether in a cradle or not. When prolonged and very tight, however, some psychologists believe that wrapping or swaddling may inhibit a child's sense of controlling his own environment.[45]

In our interviews, Kiowa and Comanche elders expressed beliefs that a child did not lose muscle tone but rather became stronger on the board because the legs pushed against the wrappings. The cradleboard may have advantages for isometric exercises.[46] On the other hand, among the Cree, children who spent the greater part of their first year bound tightly onto a board cradle showed increased incidence of congenital hip dislocation because their legs were held straight down rather than flexed.[47]

Carried on the backs of mothers or other female relatives, in close contact with other family members, babies were always included and never left alone. In this way, cradles physically and symbolically represent the closeness in families, especially between generations, as well as the importance of new tribal members.

Fig. 1.17
Ho'detaide and her children, Kiowa. The wrapped baby is one week old. Photograph by James Mooney, 1892. Courtesy Smithsonian Institution 1435B.

Who Made Cradles, for Whom, and Why: Family Ties
Creating and giving a cradle was a significant event. Not every family had a beaded cradle and not every child in a family was given a cradle, even during the period of maximal use. Most mothers simply wrapped their babies tightly and carried them on their backs in a hide or wool blanket (see fig. 9.8), and continued to do so through the mid-twentieth century. Only certain women were excellent beadworkers; among them, only a few were cradle makers.[48] People made or commissioned cradles to express love for a new life – a child born into one's own family or a family with whom one had close ties. Because women had strong reciprocal responsibilities to their brothers, the birth of a brother's first child or grandchild might occasion the gift of a fine beaded cradle. People outside the family who wished to honor a child might commission a cradle from a specialist. If an infant died, his cradle might be buried with him, in keeping with the tradition of sending prized possessions along with the deceased to comfort them (fig. 1.18). Present-day Kiowa cradle-maker Vanessa Paukeigope Jennings made a small cradle and moccasins for her sister Stevette's infant son, who died shortly after birth; she intended them to accompany the child in his burial, saying "when people leave like that, you're supposed to send them with their very best."[49]

Among the Kiowa, especially among those of status, parents or grandparents might choose certain children as *auday*, well regarded or specially favored, and make an extra effort to provide particularly fine clothing, special food, and other gifts including a beaded cradle – and generally to treat them as more privileged than others. For auday children, "horses are given away at birth, and an elaborate cradle is gotten by the parents made of buckskin."[50] An auday was often the oldest child, and very often the first grandchild, Mary Buffalo, a Kiowa woman who was herself an *auday mata'un* (favored daughter), told anthropologist Donald Collier in 1935.[51] Auday children were expected to grow up with a greater sense of responsibility toward others and to represent the ideal qualities of the Kiowa people.

Before a cradle was made, "there were prayers for thanks: for the new baby and for the material and for its gathering and use," said present-day Comanche cradle maker Weckeah (ch. 11, this volume). According to

Vanessa Jennings, a newly made cradle would be smoked and blessed with cedar and sage, and might be dedicated to one beloved person. Jennings made a cradle for the Haffenreffer Museum of Anthropology (see fig. 10.1). She dedicated it to her sister Stevette, who participated in the prayers and blessing of the cradle, but died of cancer shortly after it was completed.

Because beadworking skills were valued, the reputation of a cradle maker often endured beyond any individual cradle. Growing up in the 1920s, Weckeah constantly heard about the beaded cradle made by her grandmother Weckeah Parker, although she never saw it. Her grandfather Quanah Parker, Weckeah's husband, was a Comanche leader. The younger Weckeah has been a cradle maker from the time she was taught the skills as a child by her aunt. She spent countless hours watching and listening to older women in her extended family, who lived close to one another in a mission compound.

Jacob Ahtone recalled his mother, Tahdo, who continued to make cradles until 1938:

> Mother had no fixed work schedule, but she did work steadily and regularly on the projects. She worked five to seven hours per day and nearly every day....When at work she did not stop work when visitors came. She could talk to visitors and continue her beading.... Much of the time she was working, a daughter or granddaughter would be present to watch the progress of the work and hear stories of days gone by or receive instructions on how to live happily.[52]

Such stories are typical of the learning processes of beadworkers and other artists. In extended families, living together or in close proximity, mothers, aunts, and grandmothers taught young girls. Any interested girl was allowed to try. The older women showed them what to do, left them to work on it by themselves, and then critiqued it until, as one woman said, "it was just spot for spot, perfect."[53]

The Plains women who made the beautifully crafted cradles of the late nineteenth- early twentieth centuries had been born in the mid-nineteenth century during nomadic times, when tanning hides and shaping them into tipis, clothing, and accessories were essential skills for survival. They passed these skills on to their children through direct teaching between generations.[54] During the reservation period, a woman's role became more narrowly defined as homemaker and nurturer of

Fig. 1.18
"The Lost Child." Watercolor by Charles E. Rowell, Kiowa, 1984. H: 36 cm, W: 27 cm. When a baby died his cradle and other belongings were often placed in the grave. Courtesy Barbara A. Hail Collection.

children. As glass beads and trade cloth became plentiful, there was more time for making and decorating useful objects. As new bead-working skills developed, they were shared and passed down along kinship lines. Family relationships among beadworkers were enduring and complex (see figs. 1.21 and 9.4).

While cradles were frequently the work of an individual artist, sometimes more than one woman worked on the same cradle; often the women were related.

> This Pai-tah is a typical Indian cradle of regulation size and was made purely for service; on buckskin. The beadwork on the right hand side being worked by Mrs. White Buffalo, and donated to Mrs. Eu-nap, her sister; the beadwork on left hand side being the work of Mrs. Eu-nap, mother of Helen Ko[o]msa, whose papoose was carried in it till it became too long and then it was sold to me, known to them as Cocq-o-sone, meaning the Elktooth-man.[55]

Two sisters, the daughters of Chief Satanta, Sau'totauto (Mrs. White Buffalo) and Autoinonah (Mrs.

Fig. 1.19
Mrs. Shoshone, Comanche, has taken her child out of the cradle, which can be seen on her left. Courtesy Sam DeVenney Collection 5.

Eunap), each contributed a side to the cradle they made for Autoinonah's daughter's new baby (see page 127). In a hand-written note dated August 16, 1901, the proprietor of Stinson & Lamberson General Merchandise store in Mountain View, Oklahoma, described the sisters' cradle, probably at the request of the man who purchased the cradle from him at that time. Such documentation of family collaboration on a single cradle is, unfortunately, rare.

In another example, two women in a family of artists worked on one cradle: Paukeigope (Etta Mopope) worked with her mother Keintaddle on the cradle she is shown wearing in a photograph (see fig. 10.5). Peeking out of the cradle is her son, Stephen Mopope, who grew up to become a renowned artist.

While women made the beadwork covers, and sometimes gained fame through their artistry, men often made the boards and frames. Incising, shaping, and decorating the wooden boards that formed the lattices were usually male tasks. Some men became specialists in crafting the boards and framework, cutting and smoothing locally grown bois d'arc (Osage orange) or cedar, with hand tools, while others used commercially prepared lumber. Sam Ahtone, husband of Kiowa cradlemaker Tahdo, has been identified as a board-making specialist, who collaborated in cradle making with his wife, and also made frameworks for other women's cradles, such as those of Guohaddle (see fig. 3.1). The gendered division of labor in cradle making complicates not only the subject of "collaboration" but the larger question of identifying makers.

Becoming Known: Sale and Commodification
At the height of cradle use, full-size cradles were not made for sale outside Indian communities. Beginning in the late nineteenth century, however, women skilled in beadwork sometimes supplemented family income by selling their handiwork. As in the case of Helen Koomsa's cradle mentioned above by the general store proprietor, when a baby "became too long" its cradle might be sold. As they circulated more widely and their unique beauty attracted the attention of collectors, cradles became increasingly commodified, and their original status as gifts was permanently altered.

In 1902 Mohonk Lodge, a store sponsored by Christian missionaries, opened in Colony, Oklahoma, between Kiowa-Comanche-Apache, Southern Cheyenne, and Southern Arapaho lands. Its purpose was to stimulate the art of women in surrounding tribes, who were "among the best beadworkers in the world."[56] The store provided raw materials – hide, beads, paints, and more – at cost, in order to encourage artisans to produce the more time-consuming and difficult types of beaded objects and clothing. In turn, women who purchased the materials brought their finished products to the store for sale, and were paid in cash. Through the 1920s and 1930s beadworkers regularly obtained supplies there; the proprietor, Reese Kincaid, sold beaded objects, including toy cradles, largely through Mohonk Lodge mail order catalogs.[57] In the 1930s, one woman sold

Mohonk Lodge the cradle that had been made for her as a baby; with the money, she helped pay for her college education.[58] Family heirlooms, including old cradles, were sold there as well.

From 1917 through the 1930s Susan Peters worked among the Kiowa as a field matron, appointed by the Department of Interior to assist native peoples. Peters actively promoted Kiowa artists' work, sponsoring art education at the University of Oklahoma for a group of artists – Tsatoke, Mopope, Auchiah, Hokeah, and Asah – who became known as "the Kiowa Five," or sometimes, with Lois Smoky, "Six"; they led in popularizing the Indian art of Oklahoma. She took exhibits of fine beadwork and hidework by artists, including Tahdo and Maggie Smoky, to major collecting centers such as Albuquerque and Gallup, New Mexico. As the artistic

and monetary value of cradles grew tremendously, they were widely sought by private collectors and museums.

During the Depression a large numbers of cradles left families who found it hard to turn down a good offer. If cradles were pawned by their owners, such as at Tingley's in Anadarko, it was usually impossible for other family members to retrieve them. Many were given away as gifts to respected teachers, physicians, and churchmen. Among both Kiowa and Comanche, "if someone admired something we had, it was considered the polite thing to do to give it to them."[59]

The Arts and Crafts movement also coincided with the great period of lattice cradle making and use. Between 1880–1920, museums and private collectors competed to acquire large collections of native artifacts, especially baskets, blankets, and beadwork, as home decoration and examples of hand-crafting. Eventually many were sold or donated to anthropology museums, where they were reevaluated as ethnological specimens representing native cultures. Cradles, like other artifacts made at this time, were commodified to an extreme degree.[60]

CONTEMPORARY VISIONS AND FUTURE DIRECTIONS

Today few cradles remain in their original families. Kiowa and Comanche people are more concerned than ever about recovering knowledge about their cradles. The heightened awareness in the non-native art world of the tremendous artistic value of native people's production is another factor stimulating attention to earlier cradle-making traditions. At the same time, as contemporary artists create cradles and fine artists depict them, they gain fame.

Decorated lattice cradles are influential, primary cultural icons, although – or perhaps because – they have not been regularly used by Kiowa or Comanche people for seventy years. Conducting research for this project, I was privileged to hear Kiowa and Comanche people express reverential memories of the cradles themselves, respect for grandmothers who excelled at cradle making, satisfaction in the family bonds that learning to make cradles had forged, and pride that their people, as a group, had not only survived but produced an object of such distinction. As counterpoint to these personal stories, the photographs and written documents I con-

Fig. 1.20
A Comanche child beginning to outgrow his cradleboard has one arm outside. Note the soft rabbitskin liner. Anadarko, Oklahoma 1901. Courtesy Western History Collections, University of Oklahoma Library, Phillips 234.

sulted show that ceremonial uses of cradles continued even when daily use declined, and that although few cradles were physically present in homes, those cradles and all they stood for were held in great esteem.

In 1941, an American Indian Exposition Parade was held in Anadarko; on the Kiowa float, Kiowa girls proudly carried a lattice cradle. Grandmothers made toy cradles for grandchildren through the 1950s (see page 128). A few women made full-size cradles for grandchildren (figs. 9.6 and 9.7). Comanche families continued daily use of lattice cradles longer than Kiowas, probably because theirs were usually not beaded and were therefore lighter and more practical to carry. Comanche women also continued to use rawhide night cradles; and a few Comanche women still make them (fig. 11.1).

Families who own cradles can sometimes boast several generations of use. People often feature their cradle in photographs, holding each new child or grandchild, so that in future the pictorial record will reinforce the child's pride in his heritage. Descendants of Guohaddle keep her cradle and fleshing tools in a glass exhibit case in their living room; on the walls around it are photographs of Guohaddle, her husband, Chief Ahpeahtone, and all the children who have been photographed in the cradle since 1911.

The pervasive reverence was leavened with humor, as elders remembered that they had once, after all, been children themselves. Gina Quoetone Ware Paughty, daughter of cradle maker Daisy Mattonsaw, recalled:

> We used to play with them (the cradles) until we got caught, and we'd get a spanking, and we'd hang them back on the wall. They would tell us: "you could ruin the beads, break the beads off of there, so just handle it carefully and place it back!" So we did, but many times it was tempting to take it and just grab it and run with it![61]

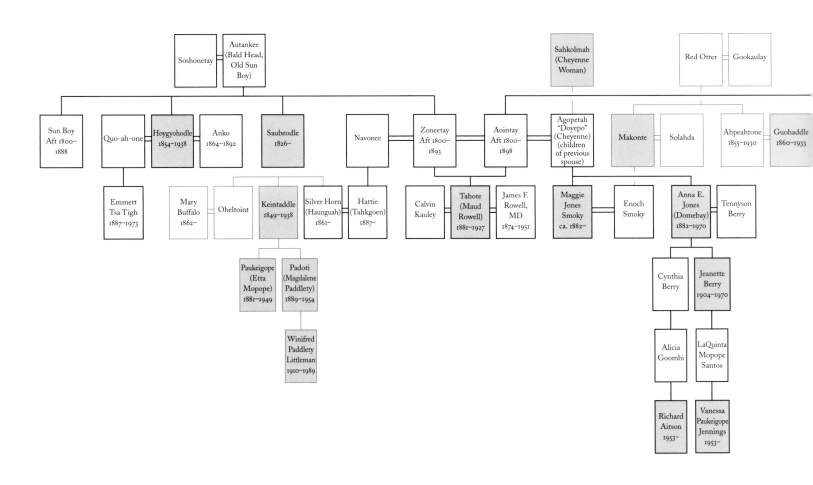

Even more than the immediate past of one's child-hood, however, the cradle is associated with the distant past, before the memory of living people. The association with free-roaming horseback life is particularly strong, so that the lattice cradle has come to stand for earlier nomadic times, although its full development was later. Twentieth-century Kiowa artists, such as Stephen Mopope and Charles E. Rowell, frequently portrayed the cradle on horseback, reinforcing that association. The cradle has also become an important gendered symbol, standing for Southern Plains women and their achievements as ledger art stands for men.[62] Today, in this as in other Plains bead art, gender divisions no longer apply. Richard Aitson, Kiowa, makes model cradles that have won awards at the annual Red Earth competitions in Oklahoma City (see page 129), and Jimmy Arterberry, Comanche, makes full-size cradles for use (see page 113).

Since the mid 1980s, Vanessa Paukeigope Jennings has dedicated herself to reviving the art of cradle making. She has made some two dozen cradles, including one for each of her grandchildren. Her cradles are used by family members as well as purchased by museums and private collectors (fig. 10.1). In keeping with earlier traditions, her husband, Carl Jennings, constructs the rawhide and wood framework and shapes and decorates the boards. Vanessa, whose grandmother and great-grandmothers were cradle makers, is conscious of the bonds of kinship and creativity. Her grandmother, Jeanette Berry, told her that she could use her family's designs and pass them on to her children. Jennings has reworked designs from Berry and from her great-grandmother Paukeigope on cradles and other objects. Her own, new designs include representational figures. She featured Saynday, the Kiowa culture hero, on a cradle she made for the Mashantucket Pequot Museum in

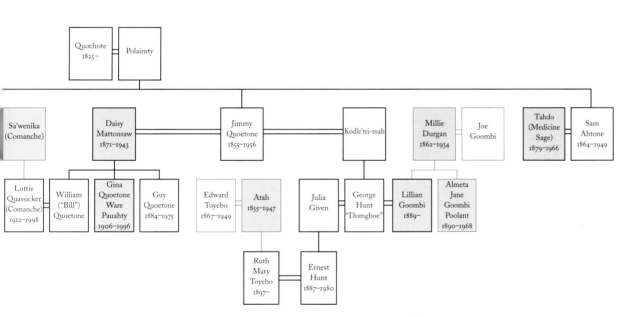

Fig 1.21
Complex extended family relationships among some Kiowa cradle makers. For example, the makers of the cradles in the Rowell Collection of the Haffenreffer Museum – Daisy Mattonsaw, Tahote, and Hoygyohodle – connect through both descent and marriage to a number of other cradle makers (see shaded boxes). Designs and techniques were passed on along kinship lines, as families worked together informally. Double horizontal lines (=) indicate marriage.

1998. Vanessa's grandfather, the artist Stephen Mopope, likewise received permission to borrow beadwork designs from his wife, Jeanette Berry, and her mother, Anna Jones.[63] He featured them in his drawings, which often depict mothers, children, and cradles (fig. 10.7).

Research for this project often raised bittersweet memories. Talking about cradles brought back the joys and sorrows of raising children and evoked long-forgotten images. A sense of loss about cradles that will be seen no more pervaded conversations. Nevertheless, people expressed optimism about the future of cradles. The corpus of information compiled for this project provides a basis for ongoing research. Many Kiowa and Comanche people have worked to re-establish the severed connections between existing cradles and those who created them. It is their hope, and mine, that as more cradles are linked to their makers, original owners, and current resting places, the cradle makers will at last be more widely recognized for their gifts of pride and love.

ACKNOWLEDGEMENTS

I wish to thank those individuals who generously contributed their knowledge to various portions of this essay: Mary Ahdosy, Jacob Ahtone, Richard Aitson, Jimmy Arterberry, Weckeah Bradley, Philip Bread, Wallace Coffey, Virginia Codynah Conwoop, Dorothy White Horse Delaune, Sam DeVenney, Ray Doyah, Georgia DuPoint, Joycetta Bear Elliott, Sharron Ahtone Harjo, Kenneth Harragara, Joe Hays, Carl Jennings, Vanessa Paukeigope Jennings, Marian Kassanavoid, Tom Kavanaugh, Benson Lanford, Lewis Lipsitt, Steve Littleman, Yancy Littleman, Carolyn Hunt Lujan, N. Scott Momaday, Juanita Pahdopony-Mithlo, Juanita Wauahdoah Nelson, Linda Poolaw, George Poolaw, Everett R. Rhoades MD, Bernadine Toyebo Rhoades, Charles Everett Rowell, EvaLu Ware Russell, Jasper Saunkeah, Ouida Sanmann, Dolores Sanmann, Beatrice Ahpeahtone Doyah Smith, Christina Hunt Simmons, Towana Spivey, Peggy Tsoodle, Josephine Wapp, and Dorothy Tsatigh Warner. For editorial insight I am indebted to Blenda Femenias, Candace Greene, David Gregg, Shepard Krech III; for genealogical aid, Natalie Moyer; for tape transcription, Kristen Holly; for technical assistance, Kathleen Luke and Janet Tanner.

NOTES

1. Linda Poolaw, videotaped interview with author, May 19, 1996.

2. Hail (1983: 143–146, 1994: 122).

3. Toy cradle, cat. no. 91.157.28, Fort Sill Museum, made by Mrs. Wild Horse in 1880s. Wild Horse was Comanche. Full-size cradle, Kiowa, cat. no. 4-5-10/63026, Peabody Museum of Archaeology and Ethnology, Harvard University. Maker unknown.

4. EvaLu Ware Russell, interview with author, July 5, 1995.

5. Anonymous personal communication to author, July 5, 1995.

6. Philip Bread, videotaped interview with author, May 20, 1998.

7. The original Kiowa homelands remain uncertain. Because the Kiowa language is related to Tanoan (both are part of the Aztec-Tanoan phylum), there may be early links to the people of the northern Rio Grande pueblos (Foster 1996: 95–96, Goddard 1996: 319). The Kiowa-Apache are Athapaskan speakers.

8. Wright (1986: 174)

9. Hail (1983: 29); see also Foster (1991), Mayhall (1971), Mooney (1979), Nye (1968a, 1968b), Wright (1986).

10. Wright (1986: 175).

11. Mayhall (1971: 263, 319).

12. Foster (1991: 81).

13. Mooney (1979: x), excerpted from a letter he wrote to the Bureau of American Ethnology after his first field trip to the Kiowa in 1891.

14. Berlandier (1969: 87) wrote these observations while on a scientific expedition for the Mexican Border Comision de Limites. His book, *The Indians of Texas in 1830,* includes Lino Sanchez y Tapia's watercolors, executed under his direction after the drawings of Jose Maria Sanchez y Tapia, the artist and cartographer on the trip. *Rancheria* is a term employed by the Spaniards meaning a "camp" or "village" (Newcomb 1961: 106).

15. For an account of the Long Expedition, see James (1966).

16. Catlin made numerous sketches while accompanying the Dragoons reconnaissance. See Catlin (1973 [1844]: vol. II, Letters 41, 42, 43).

17. See watercolor from the 1850s in Newcomb (1978: Plate 26).

18. Otis T. Mason, an anthropologist on the Smithsonian Institution staff, coined the term "lattice" to differentiate the type from the board cradle (Mason 1912: 357–359). For comparative studies of Kiowa and Comanche cradles, see Schneider (1983: 305–314) and Kavanaugh (1995). For soft cradles, see Greene (1992: 95–113).

19. *Harper's Weekly* 6(543): 329 [May 25, 1867]; sketch reproduced in Nye (1968b: 250, 251), see also Nye (1968b: 62).

20. *Annual Report of the Board of Regents of the Smithsonian Institution. National Museum Report for 1887*: 199, fig. 35; also in *U.S. National Museum Annual Report for 1894*: 508, fig. 202.

21. *Annual Report of the Board of Regents of the Smithsonian Institution. National Museum Report for 1887*: 199, fig. 34; also in *U.S. National Museum Annual Report for 1894*: 508, fig. 201.

22. A Navajo origin story tells that after a cedar tree was split by lightning, the resulting split boards were used to build a cradle, and the power of the lightning transferred to the infant as protection.

23. A travois is a horse-drawn vehicle consisting of two trailing poles serving as shafts for the horse and bearing a platform or netted cage on which was piled camp gear. The platform also carried camp members who were unable to walk or ride horses, i.e. babies, the old and the sick.

24. Weckeah Bradley, interview with author, May 21, 1998.

25. Vanessa Paukeigope Jennings and Carl Jennings, personal communication, July 9, 1999.

26. Of the 40 Kiowa and 30 Comanche cradles I have measured, the length ranges from 43″ to 47 ½″; the width from 12″ to 14,″ the height from 8 ½″ to 12 ½″. I have not found that placement of the foot of the cover corresponds to tribal preference. The Kiowa covers may look lower on the boards than Comanche covers because the long fringe often hides the lower ends of the boards.

27. In "raised outlining" the beads are sewn on in a different direction than the background or the design interior, creating a vivid contrasting edge to the design. Of the 70 fully beaded cradles I studied, 65% use an overlay stitch with raised outlining, 15% are in lazy stitch, both background and design, and 20% use a mixture of these and other stitches, including a netted stitch.

28. In about one third of the cradle covers I have studied the sides are asymmetrical in color, design, and/or stitch type.

29. The heraldic emblem may have been based on U.S. Army insignia seen at Fort Sill (see page 122). Mounted horsemen appear on a cradle in the Rhode Island School of Design Museum, cat. no. 44.610, originally an exchange with George Heye; collected from the Kiowa ca. 1917 by Col. James F. Randlett. A Southern Cheyenne bead-worker may have executed the cover but the construction is clearly Kiowa.

30. Mary Buffalo's second husband was the Kiowa artist Oheltoint, brother of the artist Silver Horn. Later photographs of her with two children in a home setting show the baby in a different cradle of typically abstract floral Kiowa design (NMNH 358404).

31. La Barre et all (1935: August 10, Heap o' Bear interview).

32. Nye (1962: 281).

33. Sharron Ahtone Harjo, personal communication, July 5, 1995.

34. Norman Feder identified a style center for colorful abstract style beadwork along the eastern Kansas/Nebraska border in the early reservation period (Feder 1965: 67–70, Hail 1983: 61–62).

35. Benson Lanford has compiled a list comparing specific Kiowa designs to Delaware and Saltillo ones; personal communication, 1997.

36. See Note 29.

37. Jimmy Arterberry, taped interview with author, May 10, 1998.

38. Jacob Ahtone, personal communication, July 1995.

39. Jimmy Arterberry, taped interview with author, June 10, 1998.

40. Gina Quoetone Ware Paughty, videotaped interview with author, June 12, 1996.

41. Beatrice Ahpeahtone Doyah Smith, interview with author, July 6, 1995.

42. Appadurai (1986).

43. Sharron Ahtone Harjo, videotaped interview, May 18, 1997.

44. Personal communications, Everett R. Rhoades, M.D., first Indian director of the Indian Health Service, and Lewis Lipsitt, Ph.D., Research Professor of Psychology, Brown University, specialist on infant and child behavior and development, May 1998.

45. Lipton, Steinscheider, and Richmond (1965); de Mause (1995: 37) also refers to their study. For other studies of cradling and wrapping, see Campos (1989), Chisholm (1983), and Gorer (1962). No such studies have been conducted among the Kiowa or Comanche.

46. Hudson (1966: 470–474).

47. Ghibely (1990) reports on a 1973–76 study in Quebec of Cree infants on the *tihkinakan*, a board cradle; and personal communication from John M. Gawoski, M.D., of the Lahey Hitchock Medical Center, Department of Laboratory Medicine, Burlington, Massachusetts, who has studied congenital hip displacement in Manitoba Cree babies.

48. Mishkin (1940) ranked Kiowa beadworkers in order of prestige gained for making certain objects. Oddly, he included as prestige objects saddles and dresses, but not cradles.

49. Vanessa Paukeigope Jennings, interview, July 3, 1995.

50. Kuito made this observation to Bernard Mishkin in 1935 (LaBarre et al. 1935: 171).

51. LaBarre et al. (1935: 95).

52. Jacob Ahtone, chapter 8, pp. 86–87 this volume.

53. Gina Quoetone Ware Paughty, taped interview with author, May 12, 1996.

54. Schneider (1982: 9, 14) discusses the importance of family connections among Kiowa artists.

55. Source file, Kiowa cradle #205285, Archives, Field Museum of Natural History, Chicago.

56. Kincaide (1939: 2).

57. Christina Hunt Simmons and Jacob Ahtone, taped interview with author, July 7, 1995. The idea for the store was first proposed by Christian missionaries at a conference at Lake Mohonk, New York, in 1898. Today the store, operating under different management, is known as Mohawk Lodge, the significance of the original name having been lost.

58. Anonymous personal communication, June 16, 1999.

59. Jimmy Arterberry, taped interview with author, June 10, 1998.

60. Jacknis (1999: 152), Krech and Hail eds; Krech (1994: 13–14).

61. Gina Quoetone Ware Paughty, interview with author, June 12, 1996.

62. See Petersen (1968) and Berlo ed. (1996).

63. Vanessa Jennings, personal communication, June 10, 1999.

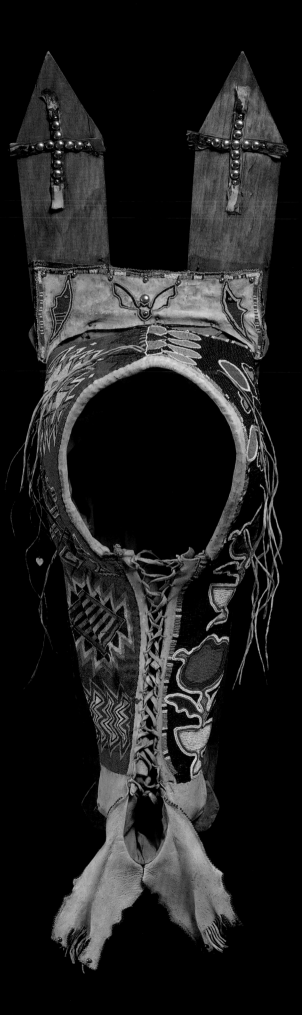

Fig. 2.1
Lattice cradle and detail of top of cover.
Kiowa, used by Maud Rowell (Tahote,
1880–1927) for her daughter Dorothy in
1903; possibly made by Maud or by one
of her mother's sisters, Saubeodle or
Hoygyohodle, both excellent beadworkers. L: 109 cm plus fringe. Native tanned
deerskin, wood, rawhide, linoleum, plain
weave cotton, yellow pigment, glass seed
beads thread-sewn on canvas, German
silver buttons, tacks and studs, silk rib-
bons; attachments: gold heart and chain,
faceted necklace beads. Unique among
Kiowa cradles in using a netted flat gourd
stitch to create geometric designs on one
side and a combination of lazy, outline,
and overlay stitches to create floral designs
on the other. Maud's brother-in-law,
E. Everett Rowell, acquired it between
1904 and 1912, in appreciation for medical
services and because of family connections.
Rudolf Haffenreffer purchased it from
George P. Rowell in 1934. Haffenreffer
Museum of Anthropology, Brown
University, Rowell Collection 61-339.
Photograph by Cathy Carver.

CHAPTER II

The Rowell Family Cradles

by EVERETT R. RHOADES

THE ROWELL CRADLES, like other Kiowa cradles, are surrounded by fascinating family histories and relationships, becoming nearly sacred family icons. In some ways, the Rowell family is even more intriguing than others, involving the marriage of a young Indian woman who grew up on the Kiowa, Comanche and Apache reservation to a physician from a prominent Stamford, Connecticut family. The Rowell family traces its origin in America to Thomas Rowell, who emigrated from England and was one of the incorporators of Salisbury, Massachusetts. The progenitor of the Stamford, and therefore, Indian Territory Rowells was Charles Emery Rowell, who studied medicine at the New York Homeopathic College and with an uncle and brother in 1880 established a family of physicians in Stamford, Connecticut. Charles's oldest son, James Frederick Rowell, was fascinated by Indians and before beginning his medical studies had visited virtually every Indian reservation in the United States and Canada, accumulating an extensive private collection of Indian artifacts.

In 1890, at age 17, he published "The Red Man", a small pamphlet for disseminating ethnographic and crafts information and for trade advertisements. James completed medical studies at Hahnemann College of Osteopathic Medicine in Philadelphia in 1895 and began a practice in Stamford. However, this was almost immediately interrupted by tuberculosis, an especially dreadful occupational hazard in those days. In a desperate

Fig. 2.2
Cabinet card portrait of Maud Rowell (1881–1927) dressed in finery in a Spanish shawl. Russell Studio, Anadarko, Oklahoma. Courtesy Haffenreffer Museum of Anthropology, Brown University 98-3-7.

effort to combat the disease, he journeyed once again to the west, seeking a climate conducive to recovery. Arriving at the end of the railway at Chickasha, Indian Territory, he was carried by wagon the forty miles to the Wichita Mountains in the heart of the former Kiowa, Comanche, and Apache reservation. Although he was not expected to survive this leg of the journey, this effort resulted not only in complete cure, but also in the establishment of a branch of this Stamford family in the Indian territory. James shared the scholarship, curiosity and entrepreneurial attributes of his father (and other Rowells) and in addition to a rudimentary medical practice (not very feasible among a small rural Indian population), he engaged in a variety of activities, becoming an Indian trader, gold miner, rancher, politician and ultimately making a considerable fortune in the Texas oil fields.

James' ancestors included Samuel, who served under General Benedict Arnold and then with Washington at Valley Forge; the famous Hannah Duston who killed her Indian captors; Elizabeth Thompson, the first woman admitted to the floor of the United States Senate (by virtue of her donation of the famous painting, "Lincoln and the Emancipation Proclamation"); George Presbury Rowell, the founder of "Printer's Ink" and considered to be one of the fathers of American advertising; and Charles Emery Rowell, the "gadfly" physician, mayor and civic leader of Stamford.

Fig. 2.4
Dr. James F. Rowell.
Courtesy Everett R.
Rhoades Collection,
from Marghrett Bean.

While the 1870–1890 Rowell family story was being written in eastern cities, one of the great Indian dramas was unfolding on the Southern Plains where Colonel Ranald S. Mackenzie at last succeeded in driving the Kiowas and Comanches into Palo Duro Canyon, Texas. There, in the fall of 1874, he burned their lodges and shot their ponies, then marched them two hundred miles on foot to Fort Sill, Indian Territory, where they settled on the reservation. In these final frontier conflicts, a prominent role was played by Chief Sun Boy (Paitahlee) and his brothers and sisters (fig. 2.3). Sun Boy was said to have been engaged in every battle the Kiowas fought from about 1840 to 1870, distinguishing himself, along with his brothers, with unusual bravery. He refused to sign the Medicine Lodge Treaty of 1867 that established the reservation in what was to become southwestern Oklahoma. His brother, Ahtotainte, one of the *Koi tsa gah* (considered to be the ten bravest warriors of the tribe), was the last Kiowa killed as the Indian-white hostilities drew to a final close in 1878. Facing starvation at Fort Sill, Sun Boy received permission to seek buffalo and during the hunt Ahtotainte was tragically shot by Texas rangers. As a result of Ahtotainte's death, and at unusual risk, Sun Boy and his remaining brothers, and a sister-in-law, Atah, left the reservation to carry out the Kiowa's final revenge "raid" into Texas.

Fig. 2.3
Sun Boy *(Paitahlee)*
"Son of the Sun,"
a renowned Kiowa
warrior who
never surrendered,
was the brother
of Hoygyohodle,
Saubeodle, and
Zoneetay and the
uncle of Maud
Rowell (Tahote).
Courtesy Smithsonian
Institution 1374B-1.

Sun Boy and his brothers had refused to surrender at Fort Sill and hid out in the nearby Wichita Mountains where family tradition has it that Sun Boy's sister, Zoneetay, would cook during the day and at night sneak out of the fort to take food to her brothers hiding in the nearby mountains.

The Sun Boy group settled in camps along Medicine Bluff Creek where it curved around the north and east bases of Mount Scott about eight miles northwest of Fort Sill. Zoneetay married a Kiowa man by the name of Aiontay with whom she had a child remarkable for her beauty. Her childhood name was Tahote (Deep Set Eyes) (fig. 2.2). Tahote, as was often the case, had other names. She was also known by the name Dodlebay, signifying great beauty and presence. Because her mother divorced Aointay before Tahote was born, and married a Comanche man by the name of Navonee (Naboni), Tahote was sometimes known by the Kiowa pronunciation: Mahbonee. Ultimately, she

took the name of an early missionary and teacher, Maud Welch, and was subsequently known by the name of Maud. Tahote, as was often the custom in those days, was at an early age given in marriage to Calvin Kauley, a member of Troop L at Fort Sill. After bearing him several children, Maud's marriage to Calvin ended and she went to live with her aunt, Hoygyohodle, near Mount Scott. Hoygyohodle (They Shot Him Up Close), another sister to Sun Boy and Zoneetay, figured prominently in Maud's life and especially in that of Maud's children. She was the beloved "big sister" to the Rowell children. While living with Hoygyohodle, Tahote made the acquaintance of Dr. James Rowell who at this time operated a nearby trading post (fig. 2.4, fig. 2.5). They soon married, thus

Fig. 2.5
The Mount Scott Red Store, run by Dr. James F. Rowell and his cousin Janette Rowell, where Maud first met her future husband. Courtesy Museum of the Great Plains, Arthur Lawrence Collection 559.

Fig. 2.6
Hoygyohodle in field with two of Maud Rowell's children, Maye Rowell and Susie Kauley, ca. 1912. Courtesy Everett R. Rhoades Collection.

establishing one of the first mixed heritage families among the Kiowas. Dr. Rowell and Maud made their home about two miles northwest of Mount Scott along what became known as Jimmy Creek, (named for Maud's uncle, Jimmy Quoetone), where they started their own family.

James' father and younger brother George took a great interest in the beautiful country around Mount Scott, visited often, and began to buy land. For a time, Dr. Charles underwrote the expenses for an intensive but short-lived search for gold in the Wichita Mountains. Together with a third brother, Dr. E. Everett Rowell, they also began to acquire Indian crafts.

THE "LOST" ROWELL COLLECTION
AND THE HAFFENREFFER MUSEUM

Just as Hoygyohodle was the beloved "big sister" to the Rowell children, on the other side of the family, the beloved uncle was James' brother, George, a graduate of Yale Law School who rapidly rose to a position of some distinction in Connecticut. George made a number of trips to Oklahoma, served as the legal advisor to Dr. James, and actively participated in the acquisition of lands, and in the acquisition of Indian crafts. George

suffered from rheumatic heart disease, which ultimately resulted in his untimely death and undoubtedly played a role in his decision to settle his collection with Mr. Haffenreffer. In addition to being an accomplished pianist, he had two major avocations: family genealogy and Indian collecting.

Dorothy Rowell, the oldest daughter of Dr. James and Maud, often remarked that her baby cradle had been given to Uncle George, along with other articles, and had been taken to the East. The family wasn't sure what had become of these materials, knowing only that George had sold his collection to another collector and that they had ultimately gone to a museum. Many years later, the noted Kiowa artist, Sharron Ahtone Harjo, (the daughter of Maud's cousin, Jacob Ahtone) was invited to exhibit in the Haffenreffer Museum of Anthropology at Brown University where she "discovered" the Rowell materials. The excitement of having found the long lost Rowell materials can be imagined. In 1985, when their daughter was graduating from Harvard, Everett (Maud's grandson) and his wife, Bernadine Rhoades, and several family members visited the museum which the curator kindly opened on a Saturday morning for the family to view the various materials. One can appreciate the emotions felt by Maud's grandchildren upon viewing these materials which had been the subject of much family discussion and speculation.

The children of James and Maud and their families have grown and had families of their own. Dorothy, their oldest child, during World War II became an elementary teacher in one-room schools throughout Comanche County and married Lee J. Rhoades of a pioneer family homesteading near Walters southeast of Lawton. Lee was an elementary school educator in Comanche County. Lee and Dorothy established their home just north of the beloved Mount Scott. Here she raised a family of five children, all of whom are actively involved in Kiowa activities. James and Maud's son, Charles Emery (named after his grandfather) became a noted artist and resides near Mount Scott. Another daughter, Maye, played an important role in tribal affairs, serving as an interpreter and member of the Kiowa Tribe's Business Committee. Subsequent generations of the Rowell family have carried on a number of occupations and professions including medicine and law. Beadwork continued to be important among Maud's Kauley children with both Mattie (Kauley) Coosewoon and Susie (Kauley) Hansen producing many beaded articles, although as far as is known neither ever produced a cradle.

Like other cradles in the exhibition, the Rowell cradles serve not only as intense vital links to a special and colorful past era but even more as intense personal links to unusual and distinctive ancestors. The emotions felt upon being able to see these articles are tempered by the feeling of satisfaction that the Rowell cradles played a significant part in the formation of the Haffenreffer Museum collection and the present exhibit.

THE HOYGYOHODLE CRADLE

Hoygyohodle was born in 1854 in what might be thought of as the pinnacle of Kiowa plains nomad life. As mentioned above, she was one of the large and significant Sun Boy relations. Especially, she was the beloved "big sister" to Maud's children and served throughout her life as a strong link to Kiowa ways (fig. 2.6). It isn't surprising that she would have made a cradle for a family

Fig. 2.7
Saubeodle, maternal aunt of Maud Rowell, in ghost dance apparel, with two of Maud's daughters: Dorothy Rowell, seated, and Mattie Kauley. Saubeodle was a medicine woman of great powers. She was also an excellent beadworker and may have made the cradle used by Dorothy Rowell (fig. 2.1). Courtesy Everett R. Rhoades Collection.

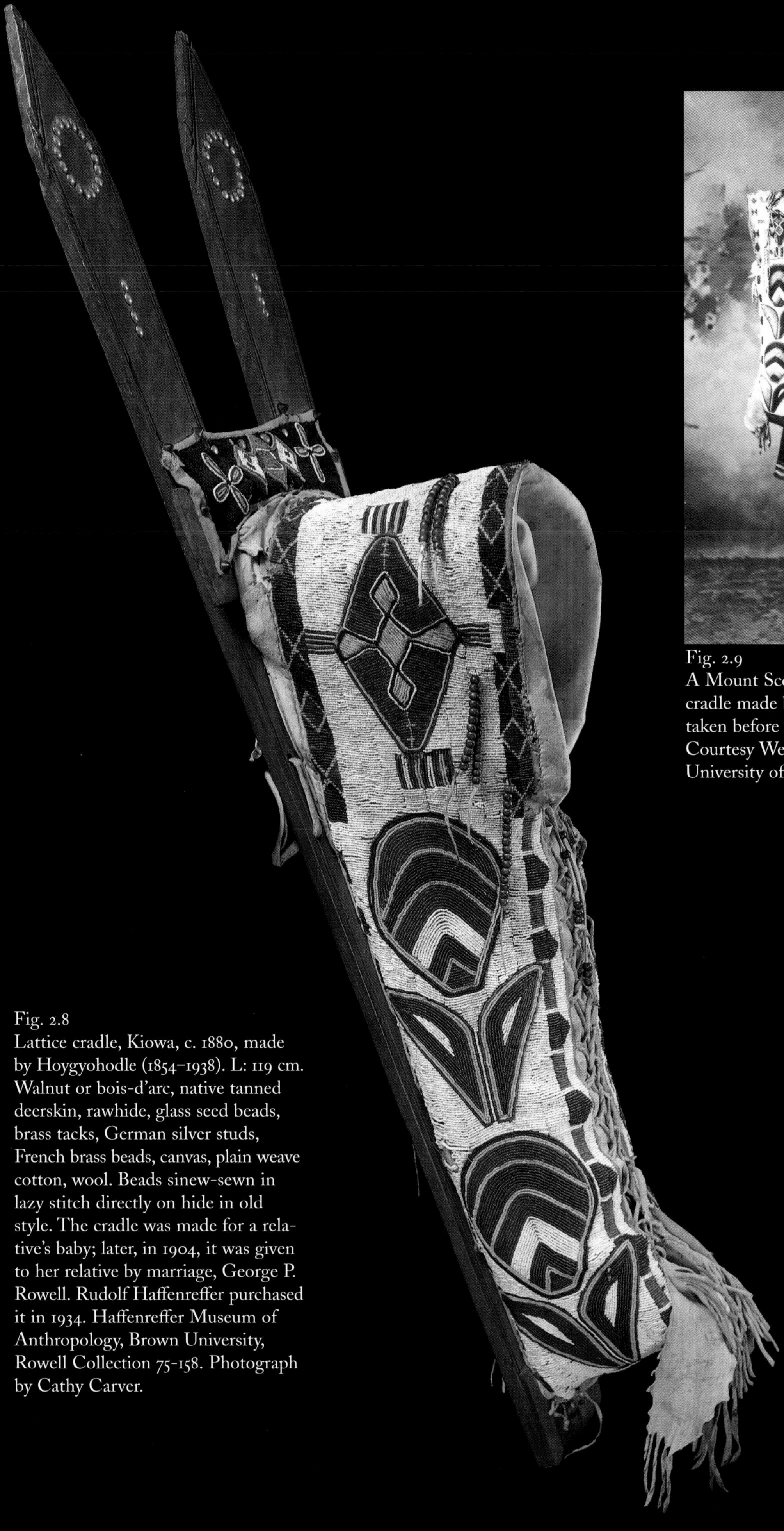

Fig. 2.9
A Mount Scott Kiowa woman with the cradle made by Hoygyohodle (HMA 75-158), taken before 1904. Russell Studio, Anadarko. Courtesy Western History Collections, University of Oklahoma Library, Phillips 921.

Fig. 2.8
Lattice cradle, Kiowa, c. 1880, made by Hoygyohodle (1854–1938). L: 119 cm. Walnut or bois-d'arc, native tanned deerskin, rawhide, glass seed beads, brass tacks, German silver studs, French brass beads, canvas, plain weave cotton, wool. Beads sinew-sewn in lazy stitch directly on hide in old style. The cradle was made for a relative's baby; later, in 1904, it was given to her relative by marriage, George P. Rowell. Rudolf Haffenreffer purchased it in 1934. Haffenreffer Museum of Anthropology, Brown University, Rowell Collection 75-158. Photograph by Cathy Carver.

member. She was married to Quoanone, a member of Troop L at Fort Sill and later to Anko, the noted calendar artist of the Kiowas. Her only child was Emmett Tsatigh, who lived on his own allotment at what is now the north entrance to the Wichita Mountain Wildlife Refuge. Hoygyohodle played a central role in the growing family of James and Maud Rowell, in Kiowa custom, becoming the linchpin of the large and busy Indian side of the family. Her home was located nearby at the northern foot of Mount Sheridan and she spent extended periods with the Rowell family who had built a house on what became known as the "Old Home Place" in the "slick hills" two miles north of Meers, Oklahoma.

Hoygyohodle and another sister, Saubeodle (fig. 2.7), a well-known medicine woman, were both noted for beadwork, and it is Hoygyohodle's handiwork that produced at least one of the Rowell cradles (fig. 2.8). This cradle, according to George Rowell's notes, was made for one of Hoygyohodle's relatives, and was obtained by George Rowell through the good offices of his brother James and his wife Maud, about 1904 or 1905. A toy cradle was later made by Hoygyohodle for the Rowell's daughter Arletta (fig. 2.11). Hoygyohodle lived a long and productive life, dying in 1938 at the age of 84 years.[1]

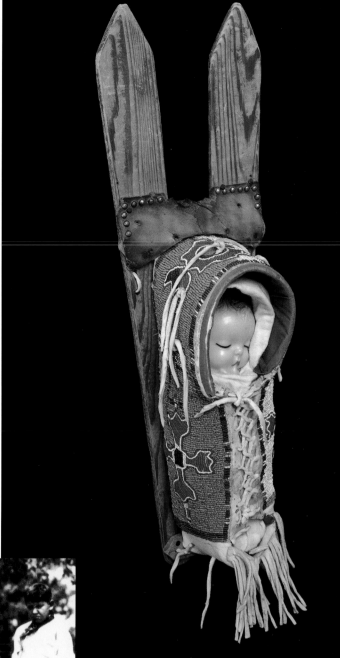

Fig. 2.11
Toy cradle, Kiowa, made by Hoygyohodle for her grandniece, Arletta Rowell (b. 1905), second daughter of Maud and Dr. James Rowell. Arletta placed the doll in the cradle in the 1930s. Arletta had no children of her own and eventually passed the cradle on to her sister Maye's granddaughter, Ouida. L: 61 cm. Pine, commercial leather bib, native tanned deerskin, canvas, brass tacks, glass seed beads in geometric designs, lazy stitch, background color blue one side, white other side; beaded medallion attached. Ouida Sanmann Collection. Photograph by Cathy Carver.

Fig. 2.10
Four children with goat cart, one holding toy cradle made by Hoygyohodle. (l to r): Two of the girls are Emma Coosewoon Chasenah and Rachel Bosin; the third is unidentified; Ernest Red Bird holds the goat cart. Probably taken in early 1930s. Courtesy Museum of the Great Plains, Sam DeVenney Collection 486.

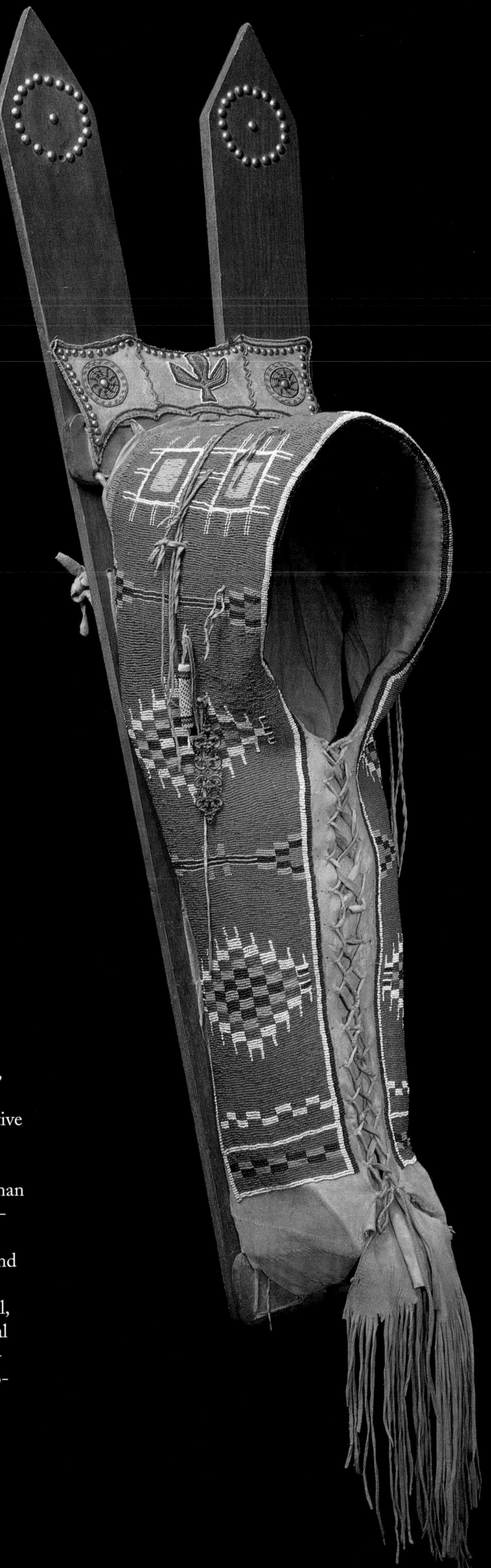

Fig. 2.12
Lattice cradle, Kiowa, made by
Daisy Mattonsaw (1871–1943), wife of
Jimmy Quoetone, of Mount Sheridan,
Comanche County, Oklahoma, 1880s.
L: 120 cm plus fringe. Oak boards, native
tanned deerskin, rawhide, glass seed
beads sinew-sewn directly on hide in
lazy stitch, separate canvas liner; German
silver buttons, nails, brass filigree orna-
ment, plain weave cotton, yellow pigment. The cradle belonged to Daisy and
Jimmy's son, Guy, who gave it to his
relative by marriage, E. Everett Rowell,
around 1912 in appreciation for medical
services rendered to one of Guy's children. Haffenreffer Museum of Anthropology, Brown University, Rowell
Collection 69-10683. Photograph by
Cathy Carver.

Fig. 2.13
Family outing, ca. 1941. (l to r): Emma Baco, Jimmy Quoetone,
cradle maker Daisy Mattonsaw, Curly, Luther Sahmount,
unknown; two boys in background are A.C. and Everett Rhoades.
Courtesy Everett R. Rhoades Collection.

THE QUOETONE CRADLE

The "Quoetone" cradle (fig. 2.12) was made by Jimmy
Quoetone's wife, Daisy, whose childhood name was
Mattonsaw (Little Girl). The Rowell collection notes for
the Haffenreffer Museum indicate that this cradle was
"made by one of the first wives of Qui-ah-tone." Qui-
ah-tone, now spelled Quoetone, is Jimmy Quoetone,
who became patriarch of a large family. However, Daisy
("Grandma Daisy" as she was known by her many
descendants) was the second wife of Quoetone and the
younger sister of his first wife, Baco (fig. 2.13). The family is firm in stating that Baco did not do beadwork.
The Quoetone cradle was made by Daisy, who made
other beaded articles, including doll cradles, for her
grandchildren. (fig. 2.14)[2]

I have many fond memories of Grandma Daisy.
My mother, Dorothy Rowell Rhoades, was very close
to Grandpa Jimmy and Grandma Daisy, on many occasions taking groceries and visiting through long and
leisurely days in the cool shade of the brush arbor that
always stood on the south side of the house. My recol-

Fig. 2.14
Daisy Mattonsaw made this cradle, shown with Ida Tsotigh
Tartsah and nephew Sherwood Tsotigh outside of the Rainy
Mountain School, Oklahoma, in the early 1900s. Note the sun
shield and other attachments no longer present. Identifications
by Roxie Tsotigh, wife of Sherwood. Courtesy Fort Sill
Museum P6401.

Fig. 2.15
Guy Quoetone (1884–1975), Kiowa, as a young boy, before going to school and having his long curls cut. Guy was dressed in fine clothes as befitted an *auday talee,* or specially favored son. Courtesy Western History Collections, University of Oklahoma Library, SWOC 175.

lections of Daisy are of an industrious woman who never spoke unkindly of anyone. She was always cooking, washing dishes, tidying up or looking after her children. Conversation was carried out in the utmost quietness, in the vigorous and melodious Kiowa language. Her son, Guy, became a Methodist minister, interpreter, and Kiowa leader (fig. 2.15). Guy gave the cradle to Dr. E. Everett Rowell in appreciation for medical services rendered to one of Guy's children.

Grandpa Jimmy was one of the prominent Kiowa headsmen of the period between closure of the reservation and World War II, widely sought as a reliable informant on Kiowa history. Even before allotments, he took advantage of government provision of farm services and accumulated large cattle and horse herds and an extensive orchard where he lived north of Mount Sheridan on the west bank of Jimmy Creek. Both the

creek and Quoetone Ridge near Mount Scott were named for him. Quoetone, a fervent adherent of the Ghost Dance, was one of the early converts to Christianity and was a driving force in the establishment of the Mount Scott Methodist Indian Mission. This church, of which Quoetone, his wives Baco and Daisy, his brother Aointay and his niece, Maud Rowell, were all charter members, still has a small but devoted congregation, many of whom are his direct descendants.

THE TAHOTE CRADLE

Much of the early story of Tahote has been related above in the description of the Rowell family. She was a dominant figure and her influence in the family continues to be felt a half century after her untimely death at age 47 years. At least in later years she was not particularly noted as a beadworker and must have made the cradle attributed to her (fig. 2.1) at an early age. There is indeed some question as to whether she is the maker of the Tahote cradle, but George Rowell was meticulous with his notes and one is usually justified in accepting the information therein.

Maud experienced a dramatic transformation from the free days of reservation life into a distinctly elegant life afforded by her husband's success in the oil business. With James, she traveled widely and was remarked to be at ease in silks and finery. She undoubtedly was the first Indian person who had her own chauffeur. During World War I she had the distinction of being a "War Mother" to not one but two sons, Casper and Gilbert. As part of the closely knit Quoetone extended family, she was a charter member of the Mount Scott Methodist Indian Mission and worked tirelessly to support the church.

FAMILY RELATIONSHIPS
AMONG CERTAIN CRADLE MAKERS

The interest in the Rowell cradles is accentuated by the interesting and extensive family relationships. Indeed, the relationships within the Kiowa tribe itself provide for hours of careful study. Several cradle makers were closely related to Maud through both her father and mother. As noted above, Daisy Mattonsaw was married to Maud's uncle, Quoetone, who was a brother to

Maud's father, Aointay. Hoygyohodle was a sister to Maud's mother, Zoneetay. Another cradle maker, Tahdo, was married to Sam Ahtone, another brother of Maud's father, Aointay. Finally, Atah, the Toyebo cradle maker, accompanied Maud Rowell's uncles on the last revenge raid of the Kiowas, and her granddaughter Bernadine Toyebo years later married Maud Rowell's grandson Everett. Such complex and interrelated family connections are characteristic of Kiowa kinships.

NOTES

1. Hoygyohodle has two surviving grandchildren, Mrs. Dorothy Warner who lives on her father Emmet's original allotment at the east foot of Mount Sheridan, and Mary Ahdosy who lives in Lawton. Dorothy was very small when Hoygyohodle was alive and has only distant memories of her. In a visit with Everett Rhoades shortly after the 1998 New Year, Dorothy recalled that Hoygyohodle always fixed Dorothy's hair very carefully, but Dorothy often preferred taking it down. Once, Hoygyohodle "put wires in" Dorothy's hair, much to the chagrin of the child.

2. One of these was made for Geneva Sahmaunt Foote, the youngest daughter of Joe Sahmaunt and Carrie Quoetone Sahmaunt.

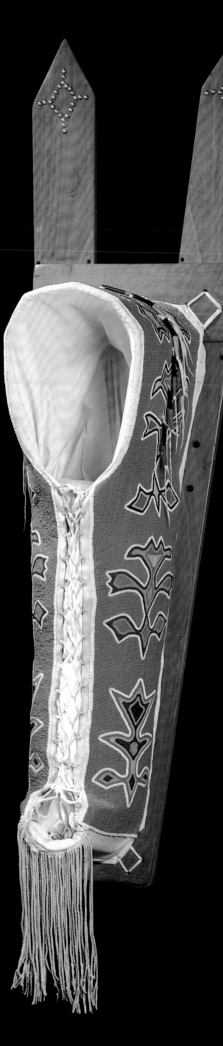

Fig. 3.1
Lattice cradle, Kiowa, made by
Guohaddle, wife of Chief Ahpeahtone
(Apiatan, *Wooden Lance*), in 1911 for her
grandson Fred. L: 119 cm plus fringe.
Cedar, glass seed beads sewn with cotton thread and sinew on canvas and
tanned deerskin; blue and white striped
cotton ticking. The cradle was put away
for many years, then restored by
Guohaddle's daughters with new lining
and with cardboard and linoleum as
stiffeners in place of the original rawhide.
It was re-mounted on the original
boards, carved by Sam Ahtone. The
leaf-like designs are symmetrical on
each side, arranged in a vertical layout
of three isolated motifs, with raised
multiple outlining. Beatrice Ahpeahtone
Doyah Smith Collection. Photograph
by Sandy Settle.

CHAPTER III

My Grandmother Guohaddle

by BEATRICE AHPEAHTONE
DOYAH SMITH

MY GRANDMOTHER GUOHADDLE (Mesquite Beans) was born in 1860 and passed away on March 25, 1933 (fig. 3.2). Her father, Iyankeah, was born in 1822 and died in 1901. Her mother was Pahtity and there is no record of her birth or death. Guohaddle was married to Ahpeahtone (Wooden Lance) who was the last recognized Kiowa chief (see fig. 4.2). Guohaddle had six children. There were three males; Geahkaygoo who died at age five, Ralph (Moppah) Ahpeahtone who was born in 1882 and passed away in 1958, and Jessie Ahpeahtone who was born in 1892 and died in 1937. There were two girls: Sahonedesah, who died at age two, and Alice Ahpeahtone, who died at age eight with no dates of their births or deaths. One unnamed infant died whose sex was not listed. When a person was born before allotment there usually were not any records kept. My grandmother had one sister that we know of. Her name was Kaubin (Big Blanket) and she was Grandpa's other wife. She had six children and they lived across the highway from us. Ahpeahtone's third wife is Asinhelah who had two children. I never knew that my grandpa had more than one wife until I was in high school. I learned that this was an accepted custom among the Kiowa, especially if the new wife was a sister to the other wife. Grandpa and Grandma were married legally by a Reverend Aitson.

Grandma and Grandpa spoke only Kiowa to each other. My mother spoke Kiowa and could understand English while father spoke Kiowa and English. When Grandma and I tried to buy things in town it was difficult to communicate. My grandma used to say, "When you grow up you can help us." Her desire was never realized because she died before I learned English.

Fig. 3.2
Guohaddle *(Mesquite Beans)* (1860–1933), Kiowa cradle maker, wife of Chief Ahpeahtone. Courtesy Beatrice Ahpeahtone Doyah Smith Collection.

Grandmother Guohaddle tanned deer hides to make the buckskin that she used. After the hides were tanned they were almost white, very pliable and pretty. I watched my grandmother tan the hides. We staked the hides so that they were not touching the ground and she let me help her spread the liver and brain mixture on them. Grandma took a hide that had dark fur and she scraped the fur off and dried it. The hide was stiff and this is what was used for the soles of moccasins and leggings. I still have the tools that she used to tan hides. In his grief, after Guohaddle died, my crippled Uncle Jessie took the tools and buried them on the property. Some years later my parents asked Jessie where the tools were and they dug them up. When I saw them later I asked if I could have them and they were given to me. They were still wrapped up in canvas the way Grandma was in the habit of storing them.

One of the things that Grandmother made was a beaded buckskin dress for my sister Lucy. She was the first born grandchild so she was special. There was a pair of beaded leggings and a belt with beaded attachments hanging from it. She made Lucy a beaded doll cradle which we no longer have except for a picture. The dress, leggings, moccasins, belt attachments and hand bag were given to my nephew's daughter. These articles belonged to my sister Wanona and she thought someone with the last name Apheahtone should inherit them. The dress, belt attachments and leggings were made after 1906, the year my sister Lucy was born.

My beaded baby cradle was made some time around 1911. It was made for my brother Fred, but the cradle was not completed in time for him to be put in it (fig. 3.3). The cradle stayed in the family until some time in the late thirties when Fred sold the cradle to my uncle Jasper Saunkeah. Uncle Jasper passed away in the fifties and my Aunt Anna sold the cradle to me. She thought we should have the cradle back in our family. The cradle had been taken apart and packed away and I asked Mother and Aunt Anna if they would assemble the cradle. They knew how to put it together and if it were left up to me, I could not do it. I had not seen the cradle made because I was born in 1918, seven years after the cradle was made. Grandmother Guohaddle was noted among the Kiowa people as being outstanding in beadworking. The cradle is now in my possession.

I stayed with my grandparents before school age and I watched Grandma do beadwork. Guohaddle sat on her bed with her legs outstretched with the beads in containers around her. She never sat in a chair at a table. She preferred to work in the sunlight from the west bedroom window. She never wore glasses and never worked at night. I used to string beads for necklaces from the beads that were poor in quality. Grandma was

Fig. 3.3
Sisters Lucy Ahpeahtone Williams (l) and Beatrice Ahpeatone in 1932 with Ralph Williams in cradle made by Guohaddle in 1911. Courtesy Beatrice Ahpeahtone Doyah Smith Collection.

a patient and gentle person and I do not remember her ever yelling at me or spanking me. The patterns that she used were mostly oak leaves. When Grandmother needed supplies for her beadwork projects we made a trip to Boakes store. The store carried needles, thread, beads and whatever else we needed. Grandpa, Grandma, Jessie and I went in a one-seated buggy for supplies. I sat on the floor in front of my grandparents. My uncle sat in the back behind the seat in a space just large enough for him. The store we traveled to was operated by the Boakes family and was located in the vicinity of Gotebo, Oklahoma, near the Rainy Mountain School.

Grandmother was 65 years old when I was born. She must have been close to 70 years old when I spent time with my grandparents. I used to dress myself and we would go to town. Mother would find us in town and there I would be with my shoes on the wrong foot. Grandma just let me wear them that way.

My grandparent's home was one mile west and a half mile south of Carnegie, Oklahoma on old number Nine Highway. Grandpa farmed the property he and Grandmother lived on. Grandpa raised cotton and feed for the horses. He also grew watermelon, cantaloupe, pumpkin, and squaw corn, and we had a lot of fruit trees. There were wild sand plums which we picked and ate fresh. Grandmother would cook the rest and dry them into patties to be eaten during the winter. We also had hackberry trees in the canyon which were great eating. When Grandpa rode across the canyon he would bring me whatever was in season: persimmons, grapes or fall plums from the trees. There was a small blackberry about the size of a peanut which we also ate and there were tiny bushes that had fruit smaller than sand plums. The Kiowa referred to these as deer fruit or apples. We also gathered skunk berries and stored them for winter use. We used these to season our corn meal mush.

My grandparent's house was easy to keep clean − real simple. It was a comfortable four room house with a porch running from the southeast to the northwest corners. We usually sat on the porch at night as Grandpa told us stories. Our house had two west rooms which only had beds in them. Clothes hung on racks nailed to the walls. The kitchen had a wood stove with an oven. There was a china cabinet in the kitchen that held the dishes. It had a work place on the front to prepare the food. There were some drawers for silverware and other things and two doors on the bottom where pots and pans were stored. There was also a square pedestal table to eat on and some chairs. The northeast room had a wood box heater. My crippled uncle stayed in this room most of the time. There wasn't any furniture in this room because we usually sat on the floor on pallets. Grandmother washed all the clothes by hand on a washboard in a tub. We had to draw the water from a well. The well didn't have a bucket and there was an oblong container with which we drew up water with a rope.

There was a large willow arbor southeast of the house and we slept outdoors under the arbor a lot. During the day there were always some men sitting under the arbor and I thought they were just visiting, but maybe it was business. Grandma and the women were kept busy cooking as they visited under a smaller cooking arbor apart from the men.

Grandmother and I used to visit an elderly woman who lived west of Carnegie by the railroad tracks. Her Indian name was Sewing Woman and she kept a girl my age who was named Sewing Girl. We played on the sand rocks while our grandmothers visited. We drove there in our one-seated buggy. It seemed so very far, but it was only a mile that we traveled. There is not a house in that area now. We went to Parker McKenzie, our 100 year old Kiowa historian, to ask who those people were and he told me Sewing Woman was related to Aileen Quoetone. Aileen is gone now and so is the old woman and her girl.

With all the work that Grandma had to do, one would wonder when she had the time to do beadwork (fig. 3.4). Beadwork is tedious and time consuming. This was a period of time that the people stayed home a lot and women sat around doing needle work and visiting. The women also did a lot of quilting together.

Grandfather, being chief, had a lot of company. There was a large coffee pot which sat on the back part of the stove in the house. Outdoors, the coffee pot sat on the back side of the fire. Visitors were offered coffee, biscuits and syrup. Sometimes when we had visitors they brought my grandparents dried meat. Sometimes it was pounded real fine. When someone butchered a cow they brought Grandpa the choice cut, maybe tenderloin. We usually ate boiled meat for breakfast, din-

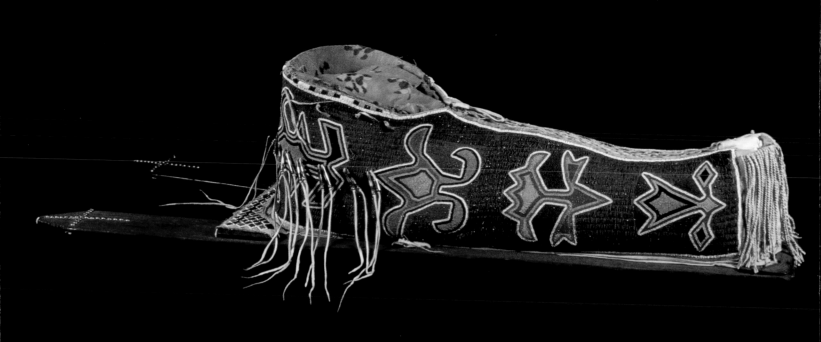

Fig. 3.4
Lattice cradle, Kiowa, made by Guohaddle, wife of Chief Ahpeahtone, 1900–1912. L: 107 cm plus fringe. Smoothed, polished wood, metal tacks, native tanned deerskin, cloth, glass seed beads, necklace beads; hide pendants, lacing, twisted fringing. Bead designs of isolated, abstract oak leaves, symmetrical on each side. Sam Noble Oklahoma Museum of Natural History, University of Oklahoma NAM 9-13-15.

ner, and supper. We also had dried fat to eat with our meals. Grandpa had relatives from the Sioux people and they would visit us occasionally. They brought us things like dried deer meat, dried choke cherries and porcupine quills. They also sent us packages from the Rosebud Agency after they returned home, but eventually, after Grandpa died, we lost contact with them.

At this period of time the elderly women took care of the babies. They always sat on the floor on a pallet. Our tents were cozy and warm, even the floor. They sang Indian lullabies to the children. We had an Indian baby swing that was attached to the boards on the windows in the house. In our willow arbor it is easy to put up a baby swing.

Our Indian people did not believe in the mother sleeping with her baby, especially when it came to nursing it. There was always the danger of smothering the

Fig. 3.5
Kiowa baby (unknown) in cradle made by Guohaddle. Courtesy Museum of the Great Plains, Sam DeVenney Collection 723.

baby. In order to keep the baby warm during the night, we "bundled" or "wrapped" it.

In the winter our house became very cold after the fires died down. We had a stove in the kitchen and a heater in the dining room. The bedrooms were very cold. When Mother used to get our little brothers ready for bed we would all be around the dining room table watching Mother wrap the babies. I remember this as being a happy time. The babies did not cry since they were getting a lot of attention. Another reason for wrapping our babies was because we mostly traveled in buggies or wagons. Even our first cars, the Model T Fords, were not too warm.

Because of the distances traveled, when people came to visit they stayed for a while. Relatives from Rainy Mountain, Saddle Mountain, Anadarko and elsewhere brought their tents and camped. People traveled in wagons so it took a while to go from one place to another. The old people were welcome to stay with anyone wherever they wished to go. Today our old people are all in rest homes.

The women did all the work in the house. That was one of our customs. Grandmother and I went after wood in the canyon. She put the wood in a canvas and carried it on her back. Grandma waited on Grandpa. After he saddled his horse to go to town she opened the gate to the yard and also the gate to the pasture which was not too far from the house. We kept the gates closed because there were cows and horses in the pasture. We followed this routine whenever Grandpa returned. My father tried to change this custom, but when he was gone we continued to wait on Grandpa.

The reason I wanted the baby cradle was to have something that Grandmother had touched. We were very close. She took me everywhere that she went and when I was small she carried me on her back. She was a tiny person, a hard worker, pleasant, and kind. Everybody liked her. Grandmother made things for others, but never had time to make me anything. So now I do have her cradle. Having a happy childhood has helped me in later years. Whenever some incident caused me to become unhappy and depressed, I would find a quiet place to sit and dwell on the happy times in my early years. This did so much for me. Somehow I felt better.

My reason for having the grandchildren's pictures taken in Grandma's beaded baby cradle is because they are descendants of Grandmother. Then too, a beaded cradle is rare. I wanted the children to see themselves in the cradle when they become older because it would have meaning for them. Every time that we put the babies in the cradle they would become so contented and fall asleep. We would think that we had to hurry and take their pictures, but they always stayed quiet, when wrapped and placed gently in the cradle.

Fig. 4.1
Lucy Ahpeahtone with doll cradle made by her grandmother
Guohaddle, with Pearl Blackstone and Mary Saunkeah (hold-
ing doll), ca. 1911. Courtesy Beatrice Ahpeahtone Doyah Smith
Collection.

CHAPTER IV

Beyond Worth

by RAY C. DOYAH

WHILE PACKING AWAY the belongings of my oldest living relative, I realized that a family heirloom was missing. Gone was a beautifully beaded lattice doll cradle made by my great-grandmother Guohaddle for a granddaughter (fig. 4.1). The doll cradle had been in the family almost a century and had been kept by different family members for their children. The missing doll cradle had fit perfectly into our collection of valued mementos made by Guohaddle.

The doll cradle was made for my aunt Lucy and when Guohaddle passed away my grandmother Ahoolah had the insight to preserve her mother-in-law's creations. I feel as if a link to the past is missing as I try to preserve the memory of my great-grandmother through the preservation of her remaining gifts. To us Guohaddle was more than a craftsperson; she was wife, mother, and grandmother who created functional gifts for the family. Her hands created the baby cradle for the first grandchild and throughout her life she made what today's society refers to as aesthetic works of art.

The doll cradle was made for the entertainment of the children – something in miniature to fit the cradle of their small arms. She also made a young girl's Kiowa buckskin dress for her granddaughter to wear for the journey into adulthood. In addition, Guohaddle made leggings, belts, purses and ornaments for the women of the family on their journey through life.

My mother was fortunate to accompany Guohaddle as she prepared the buckskin and to observe her grandmother creating inspirations from buckskin and beads. Her intricately beaded full size lattice baby cradle is the pride of our keepsakes and was made for my uncle Fred after the turn of the century. Unfortunately, Fred was too big for it when it was completed. The large lattice

Fig. 4.2
Guohaddle and Ahpeahtone with their children, Chickasha, Indian Territory. Guohaddle carries son Jessie on her back, wrapped in a blanket. Courtesy Western History Collections, University of Oklahoma Library, May Choate Collection 1.

cradle became a part of my family when mother acquired it from her aunt.

As mementos, Mom started taking her newborn grandchildren's pictures in it as she told us about its origin and tucked each child into the cradle. From my mother we learned the uniqueness of Guohaddle as Mom reminisced about sitting next to her grandmother as she beaded. Guohaddle was a master beadworker whose vision and dexterity enabled her to create intricate patterns using needle and thread. Her intuition also saw to the needs of her family as tradition guided her hands and heart to produce works of quintessential beauty.

As with most of Guohaddle's creations they were often taken out and put to use on special occasions. My younger sister was dressed in the child's buckskin dress and paraded with the doll cradle on her back in the Indian Fair parade. The doll cradle was always available for the children to play with and was used for what it was intended – the enjoyment of children.

Today I am fortunate to have my great-grandmother's legacies to see and touch and to share the product of her labors with my grandchildren. It is an honor that I am able to lay them in the cradle and have their pictures taken for a visual record – a picture of the past and present for the future (fig. 4.3). Someday I hope that my grandchildren will be able to tuck their grandchildren into the cradle and they in turn will also be told about the hands that fashioned each piece.

The lattice baby cradle is an esoteric bond within my family and represents a living history of my predecessors. The value I place on the baby cradle is inconceivable. It is beyond worth. Not only is one of our family heirlooms still intact, but I feel the essence of Guohaddle is ever present in her works. As I struggle to understand and stay in touch with my Kiowa culture, I am thankful that Guohaddle gave of herself to our family and we are able to sustain her memory by preserving her gifts of inspiration and creativity.

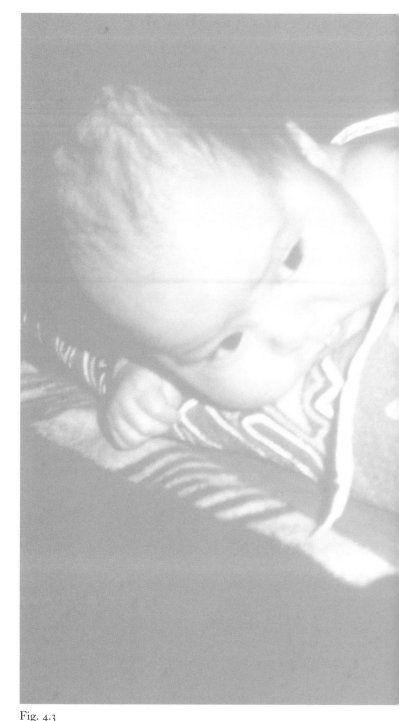

Fig. 4.3
Ray Charles Doyah II, 1994, and cradle made by his great-great-great-grandmother Guohaddle. Photograph by Ray Doyah.

Pahn-t'ope
(Cradle)

by Ray C. Doyah

"Wah-ho e-pah-shun."
before there was lightning
we felt our way
deep within my ribs
"Wah-ho e-pah-shun."

Nephew, here are my sticks
use them as you please
I will guard you
with my strength

Sister, here is my pelt
use it as you please
I will keep you dry
and laughing

Daughter, here is my sinew
use it as you please
my strength will hold you
and make you strong

"Wah-ho e-pah-shun."
hide your dark eyes
wrapped in glass oak leaves
dream where little ones dream
"Wah-ho e-pah-shun."

Brother, here is my hide
use it as you please
I will protect you
shield you from the cold

Son, here are my songs and prayers
use them as you please
they will watch over you
and keep you happy

Grandchild, here are my decorations
use them as you please
my symbols will protect you
make your journey safe

"Wah-ho e-pah-shun."
nourish the world for me
swallow my milk
nourish the earth
"Wah-ho e-pah-shun."

"Wah-ho" is the singsong lullaby
which I heard most often. Mom
said that it was sung while rocking
the baby and the five syllable
verse was repeated over and over.
I added "e-pah-shun" (little baby)
in place of "tah-lee shun" (little boy)
and "mah-tawn shun" (little girl).

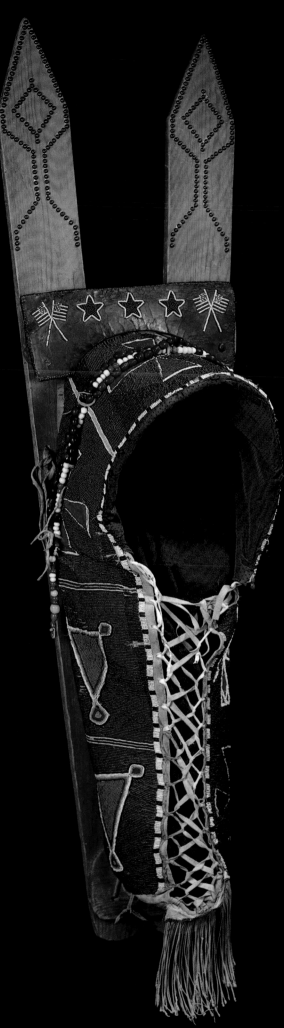

Fig. 5.1
Lattice cradle, fully beaded,
Comanche, 1890–1910, attributed to
Toquode (Toquoaty). L: 120.5 cm
plus fringe. Boards show traces of
red-purple pigment, outlined with
tacks; cover fully beaded glass beads,
designs abstract and geometric, asymmetric on sides, with 4-directional
motifs either side of head area; bib
of commercial leather, beaded with
crossed flags and stars. Early photos
show a *si'wuparu* and a different bib
and boards. Pahdopony Family Collection. Photograph by Sandy Settle.

CHAPTER V

Comanche Cradles: Carriers of Tradition

by PAHDOPONY

SOUTHERN PLAINS COMANCHE INFANTS fully viewed the world from their cradles. Infants were carried in an upright position, tightly wrapped, and laced into an elaborately designed and sometimes beaded Comanche cradleboard.[1] In contrast to Euroamerican infants whose view of the world was supinate in a usually stationary crib, Comanche infants, who were carried at eye level, saw and heard the world of their families very early.

Tsomo waakohno or *tᵾrokohno* is the Comanche term for a fully beaded or "fancy" cradleboard (figs. 5.1, 5.2).[2] Not all babies had a fully beaded cradleboard; only certain families had them, and these carriers were used when babies "went to town."[3] Almost identical to tsomo waakohno but lacking beadwork was the *waakohno (waak)* which translates to "unbeaded cradleboard with cedar points" or "cedar carrier" (fig. 5.5). Some waakohno were painted with geometric designs similar to beadwork patterns that appeared on the elaborately beaded tsomo waakohno. Waakohno were more common for everyday, possibly because of the time and materials required in the creation of a fully beaded cradle. This carrier was covered in buckskin and later, canvas. Although it was not as ornate as a fully beaded cradle, individual artistry and construction were still considered masterful and just as functional. Metal tacks arranged in a symmetrical pattern decorated the cedar support points above both tsomo waakohno and waakohno. The women of the family carried either of these cradles to public events such as shopping trips, social dances, or any social gatherings attended by families.

Historically, Comanches of the Southern Plains were nomadic hunters; therefore, rawhide and leatherwork were important resources of everyday life. A very

Fig. 5.2
Toquode (Mrs. Mamie Kiowa Carpio), and her husband Sam Carpio with their grandson Rusty Simmons in the cradle she made. Courtesy Sam DeVenney Collection 13.

early simple rawhide cradle preceded both tsomo waakohno and waakohno. It was called the *haabikɨno* and was made of a single piece of rolled rawhide, sturdy, curved, with a round-shaped head support and a footrest, laced from bottom to top, with no decoration (fig. 5.3). It was used to provide support and protection for newborns. Many Comanches today describe these simple rawhide cradles as "day cradles" or "everyday cradles" possibly because they were not highly decorated. Still other Comanches refer to these rawhide constructions as "night cradles" because infants slept in them at night. Most everyone had the rawhide haabikɨno cradle. It was compact, easy to carry, and it enabled a mother to nurse her child discreetly while in public. Comanche women's dresses, whether they were earlier buckskin or later cloth dresses, were designed to open from the armpit to the wrist. A shawl draped over the shoulder or wrapped around the waist further emphasized modesty and gave mother and child relaxed privacy even in crowded public places. Very few observers would be able to determine if an infant were being nursed by its mother if she

Fig. 5.3
Mr. and Mrs. Donald Big Cow with child in *haabikɨno*.
Courtesy Sam DeVenney Collection 14.

draped her buckskin fringes, cotton sleeve, or shawl over her child in a rawhide cradle or cradleboard.

After the introduction of European glass beads to the Southern Plains, and when settled life on reservations made trade beads easily accessible, beaded cradleboards with cedar points were made. These beaded cradles could be carried on an adult's back and supported by a thick leather strap across the chest. The cradleboard's weight was evenly distributed as it rested against hips and shoulders. Although a cradleboard may stand four feet tall from bottom to top of cedar points, it was relatively lightweight.

Although all members of the family interacted with infants in some way or another, grandmothers, aunties, sisters or other females might sing lullabies, carry infants in cradles, talk softly to them, touch them, or give them tastes of different foods. Several Comanche sources remember seeing women carrying cradleboards in public but none recalled seeing men carrying them in public. Males might admire infants, lift them up briefly (in public) and talk to them, but females generally were the primary caregivers of infants during this period of time. Because their infants were in cradleboards, the care-givers had free hands to participate in everyday chores, conversations, and general activities of the work day. Males of the family often assisted in the construction of the cradles, as for instance, in making the cedar points, but they became much more involved once infants were past the cradleboard stage.

Comanche people are by nature highly social beings. It was most natural for infants to be included in everyday activities. These tiny passive observers could be seen and admired, carried at adult eye level. Today, culturally connected Comanches continue to wrap their infants tightly in a blanket shortly after they are born. A few babies may struggle and protest for a short time, but to Comanche people, this is the most natural state for infants. It is at this time that tiny infants can be laced up into a haabikɨno. Infants might remain in these rawhide cradles at times during the day and sleep in them at night. Haabikɨno were easily accessible, lightweight, transportable, and common.

Medical research has shown that newborn infants thrive better if they are kept in close proximity and form an attachment with the parent and thus foster a sense of well being.[4] Comanche infants were enveloped in a snug and warm structure rather than tossing and twisting about freely.[5] This is information that Comanche people knew intuitively, that infants need to continue to feel the same snug structure that they knew *in vitro*. The physical closeness of the cradle is important to infants. In several instances, non-Native people have inquired, "Are Comanche children physiologically delayed by the experience of being in a cradleboard?" The answer is no, resoundingly, no! Comanche children suffered no ill effects from being in a cradleboard; in fact, they probably thrived as the center of attention. Babies were not left in cradleboards for inordinate amounts of time. They were taken out of the cradles often, just as today's mothers use plastic infant carriers, car seats, and portable cribs interchangeably for their infants.

Once infants were large enough to be supported in a cedar pointed waakohno, usually two to six months of age, they remained in it for varying lengths of time. Before cloth was commonly available, dried natural moss was wrapped around infants and used as diapers as infants were carried in cradleboards. Moss was abundant. It was also clean, fresh, absorbent, and biodegradable. Other materials that might have been used include soft buckskin and, later, cotton "flour sack" material. Infants were kept dry and clean. Comanche sources agree that the cradleboards were for either males or females; however, a notched leather shield *si'wuparru*, which could be laced on to the cover at the bottom of the cradle, always indicated that it was in use by a male infant. Its purpose was to deflect urine away from the cover. According to Weckeah Bradley, a Comanche elder and cradle maker, it "was very easy to potty train little boys" by making a "pssssssssst" sound, while gently tilting the cradleboard forward.[6] The leather shield could be easily removed if a female child were to use the cradle.

Cradleboard construction might have begun once a forthcoming birth was announced.[7] Men crafted the "cedar points" or boards, sometimes from the tree itself, and sometimes, according to Comanche elder Lavina Chasenah-Mithlo, using ready-made lumber from abandoned wagons. Women beaded the cradles. Fully beaded cradleboards took months of construction. Once a fully beaded cradle was made, usually all mem-

Fig. 5.4
Toddler Howard Pahdopony (b. 1915) guards his cradle. As the oldest brother he used the cradle first, followed by his brother Sam, and then by a cousin, Stacy. Courtesy Sam DeVenney Collection 12.

bers of the family had access to its use. Often a cradle would be passed down through several generations in a family. Comanche cradleboards were generally made for the firstborn. In the case of the Pahdopony cradleboard, Howard Pahdopony was the first to use it, and then it was used by my father, Sam Pahdopony, who was Howard's brother (fig. 5.4). My father has spoken of the firstborn male in his family: "he was the king!" Later, Stacy Pahdopony, who was the first male cousin, used it. Comanche people have been quick to disagree with earlier written accounts that cradleboards were a

Fig. 5.5
Toy lattice cradle, *(waakohno)*, and doll,
Comanche, ca. 1880. L: 89 cm. Wood,
hide, canvas, small gourds, shells, hawk
bells, glass beads around head area.
Philbrook Museum of Art, Ellis Soper
Collection 1995.24.115 a,b.

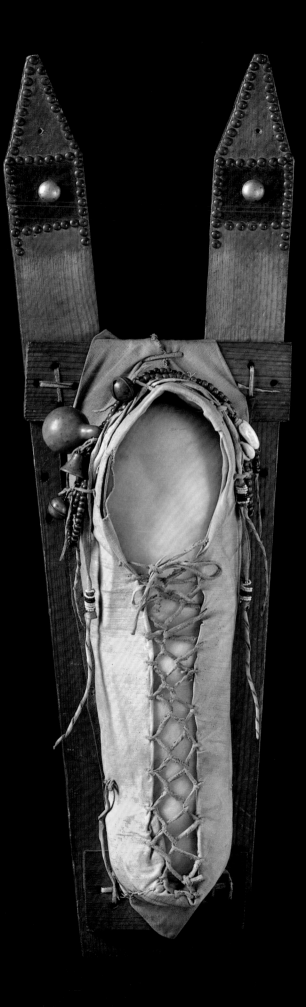

sign of wealth for the people. Comanche sources agree that the non-Native concept of wealth didn't necessarily fit the Numunᵘᵘ (Comanche) concept of wealth. Cooperative societies were generally non-competitive and, even today, a good sign of wealth is the ability to help others. For example, as not all families had an elaborate and fully beaded tsomo waakohno, it was common for those who had one to lend it out to others for formal portraits[8] (fig. 5.6).

I have wrestled with two issues on the research for this article and exhibit. I have considered the "protectiveness" of the Comanche people for information that many elders feel "belongs to the People." After all, what more can be taken from the People? How will this information be used? Who will have the information? As an educator and also as an advocate for the underrepresented and under-served of our native populations, I have decided that the information has to be preserved. It has to be shared. The future generations of Comanche people have the right to have the information. Also, the exhibit has been steadfast in the authenticity and presentation of information. Many elders remember the past, when our histories were sanitized and written for us. Interpretations were made with no value given to the "oral" traditions of the people. Yet today, I do see an appreciation for information from the people. Today, we have the "tools" to write our own histories, interpret ourselves, and tell our own stories. This is the contribution of the essay "Comanche Cradles: Carriers of Tradition."

The Comanche of the Southern Plains used family designs that linked them to their tribe and identified them as individuals. Symbols and designs had meanings interpretable to that individual or to his or her tribe. Jerry Ward, a Comanche artisan, has described the different artistic expressions of men and women: "in Comanche culture women painted on tipis and the designs were usually geometric, but when men painted, the designs were about war exploits, horse stealing, or an animal that gave them their medicine (strength)."[9] Since women beaded the cradles, cradle designs were usually geometric. A pictorial language developed as an expression of the essence of family or tribal identity. Some examples from the Pahdopony family cradle cover are in a variety of central hourglass forms, and

Fig. 5.6
Mrs. Perkaguanard, known as "Old Lady Tuu-saa-se (Tisarcy)," Comanche, was the great-aunt of Sam Pahdopony and great-grandmother of Sam DeVenney. She is shown here with Esa Attocknie (b. 1954) in the cradle attributed to Toquode. Courtesy Museum of the Great Plains, Sam DeVenney Collection 824.

also cross designs with wide flat ends representing the sacred four directions. Both were common in traditional, late 1800 Comanche designs.

Another common geometric symbol was the circle. Although not represented in the Pahdopony cradle, it was common in beadwork and painted design. The circle often represented the sun or "centeredness." Centeredness was an almost universally native holistic concept. Staying in balance was the goal. Good was the opposite of bad, but "centeredness" was the best concept. To be neither on one side or the other was favored.

Although the design pattern on the Pahdopony cradle cover is generally asymmetrical, there is a balance and harmony in the overall beaded patterns. The background color is predominantly beaded in a deep blue, which was a favorite and common Comanche color choice. It did not imply a necessarily "male" color. The cover has accent patterns containing red, white, and a small amount of yellow. The blue background color is, upon close inspection, varied in blues. It has several areas that appear as if the artist began in one blue, and ended in another blue; however, the "different" blue is worked into an asymmetrical pattern that is pleasing to the eye. Perhaps the artist ran out of a particular bead color, and noted that a fairly close color of blue existed on a worn out pair of moccasins. As adapters, the Comanche woman simply took apart the worn moccasins and reworked the beads into a new cradleboard. My mother, Marjorie Tahmahkera-Pahdopony, related a story of her grandmother who repaired a pair of old worn out "store bought leather shoes" with new rawhide moccasin soles. The "new" shoes were then everyday house shoes![10] I can only imagine what they must have looked like.

Comanche people were economical in everything they did. There was no waste. If leather wore out, it could be replaced. Beads could be lost, but rarely worn out, and could be used and reused again and again.

The commercial leather bib or head piece on the Pahdopony cradle, with crossed United States flags at either end and three blue stars outlined in white borders, was added after 1915, possibly in honor of a World War I soldier. The Comanche were traditionally a warrior society. Appreciating the symbolism of the flag as a military standard they sometimes incorporated flag motifs into their more usual repertoire of geometric bead designs. The red mescal beans and blue and white trade beads were sewn to the top of the cradleboard and designed to be untied and lowered to the eye level of a child for his or her visual pleasure (fig. 5.7). The right side of the cradle cover has a unique pattern that appears to be a geometric adaptation of a stylized bird with outstretched wings or perhaps a representation of an oak leaf. Its white outline contrasts highly in color with the blue background.

Through the years, I have spent countless hours absorbing the intricate beadwork making up the simple yet intricate geometric patterns. I have admired the careful and persistent handiwork that demonstrated an obvious love for colorful artistic contrast. I have observed the natural and human-made materials of glass, leather, wood, metal, mescal beans, canvas and cloth, that made up the cradleboard, and concluded that my ancestors were adapters; they were survivors, and they influenced who we native people are today. Suzan Shown Harjo has described native peoples of America as "the children of cultural magnificence; the parents of the visions and dreams of our ancestors. We are the modern evidence of our ancient continuums."[11]

The poem (facing page) presents an image of my family and the Comanche elders who can remember the cradles when they were in common, active, everyday use. It represents the knowledge, wisdom and power of those elders who can remember the lost information that we younger people can never recapture because we are busy adapting to new ways and culture. We are survivors and we are adapters too.

In summary, Comanche cradles were carriers of tradition. They bound the people to a culture in which "the People" represented the richest resource. When a child was carried in a cradleboard, it signified honor, patience, respect, love and the belief that the culture would continue. A child in a cradleboard was a blessing to the viewers because each individually sewn bead, rich color, and design symbolized the richness and artistry of Comanche culture at its very best.

NOTES

1. The terms cradle and cradleboard are used interchangeably in this article to refer to cradles of lattice-type construction.

2. All Comanche translations from Comanche Language and Cultural Preservation Committee: Edith Gordon 1999.

3. Lavina Chasenah-Mithlo, Comanche elder, interview with author, 1998.

4. Waldo E. Nelson, M.D. *Textbook of Pediatrics*, 15th Ed., (W. B. Sanders Co. Philadelphia, 1996), 30–31.

5. Weckeah Bradley, interview with author, 1998.

6. Weckeah Bradley, interview with author, 1998.

7. Weckeah Bradley, interview with author, 1998.

8. Sam Pahdopony, Comanche elder, interviews with author, 1998.

9. Jerry Ward, interview with author, 1990.

10. Marjorie Tahmakera-Pahdopony, interview with author, 1998.

11. Suzan Harjo, *Native Peoples Magazine*, Fall/Winter 1994, (Phoenix).

Fig. 5.7
Robert Michael Hausman, Comanche (b. 1972), smiles from
the cradle used by his family for three generations. He is
the son of Juanita Pahdopony-Mithlo and Dan Hausman.
Courtesy Juanita Pahdopony-Mithlo Collection.

Comanche Elder Wisdom

It has taken a lot of years
for my father
to share his culture with me
Pu?nepeta
who was not born a warrior
though born warrior-like
moves slowly into their circle
animal-like
so as to not create
a ripple in the waters,
so as to not disturb
the delicate balance,
sensing the power
of the group, the strength,
the utter capacity
to cut to the quick,
the power to disarm and
change minds
with wisdom,
the power to capture
or captivate, or maybe
the power to reduce a warrior
to tears
by simply saying softly,
Tutaa
Listening to the murmuring voices,
her eyes cast downward
in absolute respect,
she hears an elder state
in familiar Comanche language,
"Whose daughter is that?"
The answer defines her perfectly,
in their generation,
only a lifetime ago,
what this generation cannot do;
instead we question,
"What tribe are you?"
Because our circles are larger now
these rich tapestry, quilt piece-work thoughts unravel slowly
with the sovereign and divine knowledge
that these elders are my people,
as I walk slowly through the rows
of the long tables at lunchtime
at the Comanche Elders' Nutrition Center.

Pahdopony '93

(Pu?nepeta: the "only" daughter
Tutaa: expression of endearment; comfort)

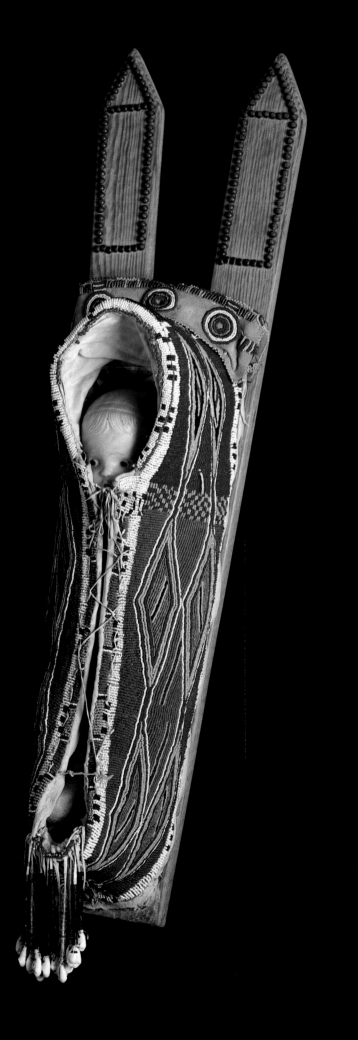

Fig. 6.1
Toy lattice cradle, fully beaded,
Kiowa, made by Atah (Mrs. Edward
Toyebo), Mountain View, Oklahoma
for granddaughter Julia Given Hunt
Geiogemah ca. 1928. L: 75 cm plus
fringe. Wood, brass pins, tanned
deerskin, sinew, cotton thread, canvas; hide lacing, bib; muslin lining;
hide fringe beaded, ending in cowrie
shells; glass seed beads, sewn in
overlay and Crow stitch with white
outlining of motifs, in continuous
design of elongated, connecting
diamonds on both sides of cradle
and around head, in yellow, green,
blues, pink. Blue background on
sides; red around head. Christina
Hunt Simmons Collection.
Photograph by Derek Jennings.

CHAPTER VI

Memories of Atah

by BERNADINE HERWONA TOYEBO RHOADES
(Tosahnhaw, Coming Home)

ATAH WAS BORN in Indian Territory in 1855 and died April 12, 1947 at the age of 92 years (fig. 6.2). Her father was Sittawyeahty and her mother was Iotapetay. Her mother died while giving birth to Atah. My father told me that Atah became an orphan upon her mother's death, so I assume her father preceded her in death. She was then raised by her uncle, Kodaybohone. There is a town in western Oklahoma named for him, Gotebo, Oklahoma. His sister, Omebo, also helped to raise her. My father, Charles Toyebo, said that she thought of them as her parents and spoke of them lovingly. She called Gotebo her father.

In the Kiowa tradition, your mother's sister is called mother and her brother is addressed as uncle. Your father's brother is called father and his sister would be your aunt. Your cousins are called your brothers and sisters. The paternal grandmother is addressed as *tahlee* and your maternal grandmother is *than-tay*. Grandfathers are called *kohn-tay*. Atah was my tahlee. At a large Kiowa gathering a person can have many mothers, fathers, uncles, grandparents, brothers and sisters present. It is a good feeling. You know you have a lot of love and caring. It is the Kiowa way.

Atah was married twice. Her first husband was Setmauntay (Bear Hand). My father told me she was a young girl when she married. They had two children. The children became ill with smallpox and died on the same day. They were buried together in the same grave. It must have been a sad time for my grandmother.

Toyebo (Outstanding) was my grandmother's second husband. He was my grandfather (fig. 6.3). Atah and Toyebo had four children, Lewis (Tsodlekoy), Milton Toyebo, Ruth Mary Toyebo Hunt and Charles (Kauty) Toyebo, my father.[1]

Fig. 6.2
Atah (1855–1947) wearing high legging moccasins. Courtesy Christina Hunt Simmons Collection.

Fig. 6.3
Atah and her husband, Edward Toyebo. Courtesy Christina
Hunt Simmons Collection.

Atah was a small woman and exuded a lot of energy. She was in her 70s when I was born in 1931. Her bead-working days were at an end because of failing eyesight. I did not observe her at beadworking, but I have been told of her busy life. My sister and brother and some of our cousins were fortunate to have observed her doing the beadworking. They were recipients of her finished products. Atah was a prolific beadworker. She prepared the hides for the moccasins and leggings she made. She scraped the hair of the hides and prepared them for use as soles of the moccasins. She made cradles for her children and for her grandchildren (fig. 6.4). She also made doll cradles for some of her granddaughters.

Tahlee's granddaughters Carolyn Lujan and Christina Simmons remember that she was a very busy and industrious woman. She was always working on

some project. They accompanied Tahlee sometimes when she went to purchase beads and beadworking supplies, probably to Clinton, Oklahoma which is in Cheyenne country. They observed her preparing the hides. Atah staked the hides to the ground so they could be scraped with a tool and then rubbed the skin with blood or cow brains to soften it. She kept a cloth on her lap to wipe any excess off before it stained the skin. This process probably took a lot of time before the skin was ready to be worked. Christina still has a cradle that Tahlee made. It still has the doll in it (fig. 6.1).

Evelyn Longhorn, my sister, tells of observing Tahlee making doll cradles for her and our sister, Wanona, now deceased. Tahlee used strips of canvas and red beads on Wanona's cradle and turquoise-colored beads on hers. The back boards of the cradles had silver-colored nail heads decorating them. She said that Tahlee told them "All good, well-to-do Kiowa girls have cradles and that is why I am making these for you." Evelyn does not know what happened to them. She suspects they were pawned because she and Wanona saw them in a pawn shop window in Oklahoma City. They tried to buy them back but the price was too high. The owner told them the cradles were purchased from a collector. Many cradles and other beaded articles found their way to the pawn shop. My father told us that there was a cradle of his mother's at the Smithsonian in Washington, D.C. I don't know if it is still there.

Delores Harragarra, another granddaughter, said Tahlee made a small teepee for her out of a thin fabric. She made a parfleche on which she painted designs and painted a backrest. These items were scaled to size with the teepee.

In addition to beadworking, Atah also made cowhide vests. My brother, Carlos, tells of one given to him by Tahlee. Christina tells me that Tahlee always made one for a young boy at church. Atah was a busy woman. She assisted in the butchering of cows for meat. The meat was dried because there was no refrigeration. She dried everything – meat, berries, and organs of the cow such as the lungs. Some of the dried meat she pounded until it was almost a powder, along with berries to sweeten it a bit. It was kept wrapped in a white cloth and she shared it with us when she wanted to give us a treat. It is called *same-kkee*. It is very good to eat, but meat nowadays very seldom is dried in this fashion. Dried meat soup is especially delicious to me. Tahlee's biscuits are still remembered with affection. Today, biscuits are judged by how high they can rise and how fluffy they can be. Tahlee's were not very high, but I loved them. Some of my family could probably say that I inherited the talent of making flat biscuits. I wish I had one of her biscuits today.

My tahlee not only could skin hides, make them soft, do beadwork, make all her own moccasins and leggings, dry food, and take care of the household, but you could probably also add a little painkilling to her talents and knowledge. Delores Harragarra tells of the time Tahlee came to visit. Dee was suffering with a toothache when Tahlee and Grandpa came. Tahlee went out into the pasture, found a plant, pulled it out of the ground,

Fig. 6.4
Lester Floyd Toyebo in cradle made by Atah, with Mary White Horse, ca. 1911. Courtesy Richenda Toyebo Collection.

cleaned the root and chewed it. She then applied it to Dee's gums and deadened the pain. Tahlee was also present when Delores was born. She and Martha Doyeto were the doctor's nurses. When the doctor was weighing the baby, Martha said that Grandma put her hands underneath the scales in case the doctor dropped her. Tahlee was forever watchful.

Atah and Toyebo were allotted land near Mountain View, Oklahoma very near a place called Rainy Mountain. They lived in a two-story house several miles west and south of town. You had to cross what is known as Big Tree's Crossing to get to it. A wooden arbor was built near the house where most of the summer days were spent. It had two screened rooms, I assume for a kitchen and dining area. Even with all the outdoors at their place, Atah preferred the arbor to an enclosed house. Ioleta Hunt McElhaney, sister-in-law to my Aunt Mary Toyebo Hunt, once came to visit them.[2] She and my father arrived at the same time and they did not find Tahlee or Grandpa in the house. They heard voices and went to the west side of the house. When asked why they were outside, Tahlee said the house was too confining. Carolyn Lujan said that many times in the dead of a cold winter, Tahlee would have Grandpa set up the canvas wall tent and there they would sleep contentedly.

Tahlee was also a marvelous story teller. Several of my summers were spent with her and Grandpa. There was no electricity, gas or running water. If you can imagine a world without all these things, you can also imagine a world without television and radio. A person might imagine that world as very boring, but to the contrary, it was a very exciting time for me. At the end of a busy day watching Tahlee and Grandpa do their chores, maybe a trip into Mountain View in the wagon or in a one-horse buggy, it would be time for supper. Then it would be bedtime and that meant story time. I slept with my grandparents and Tahlee would begin her stories. She told Saynday stories, the *auday* (special) *mata'un* (girl) story and others. I especially liked the story about the little girls that were playing and one put on a bear skin and became like a wild, mad bear. She chased her sisters and a rock called out to them to stand on him to be safe. Each time the bear reached for them, the rock would grow taller until the mad bear could no longer reach them. This is a very shortened version of a story about what is known today as Devil's Tower in Wyoming. There are many versions of this story, but this is what my grandmother told me and that is how I remember the story. We have visited Devil's Tower and each time it is as moving as the first time I saw the rock formation.

The most exciting story of them all was the one she told of her own real life adventure. The story of when she accompanied her first husband, Setmauntay, and others into Texas to avenge the death of his brother, Ahtotainte.[3]

In the spring, April to be exact, another brother, Pahgotogoodle, gathered a group to conduct a revenge raid to avenge the death of his brother because nothing had been done to punish the Texas Rangers who committed the killing. There were thirty-seven men in the group and one woman, my tahlee, Atah. A medicine man was consulted and a white owl came to give them instructions as to what to do. They were to go to the place were Ahtotainte was killed, in Texas. They had to sneak off the reservation in order to do this. They were instructed to kill only one white man. No other person was to be harmed. The owl was very specific about this. When they reached the place where Ahtotainte was killed they spotted a man on horseback and two in a wagon. They pursued only the man on his horse. They killed him. The two men in the wagon unhitched the team of horses and rode away very quickly.

Tahlee told how they were chased. I could almost hear the pounding of the horses' hoofs pursuing them. My understanding was that women were not usually on this kind of raid, and to imagine my grandmother being chased was a little scary. Again an owl came to advise them as to what to do. They hid under a bluff of some sort and a big sandstorm came so they could not be detected. The owl told them to become very still and not even the horses were to make any kind of sound. The instructions were followed and my tahlee lived to tell us this tale. I remember feeling very grateful to be able to feel her warmth next to me gazing out at the night. I don't know if my grandfather stayed awake but I did and so did my younger brother, Buddy.

The things in the wagon were taken as war trophies and my grandmother chose a coffee grinder. My sister, Evelyn Longhorn, was given two Kiowa names commemorating this event. Tsoimahkoongyah (Coffee Grinder) and Gyahhonedomei (Went on the Last Raid) were the names bestowed on her by our tahlee.

Atah experienced many changes in her life. She was a witness to the end of life on the prairie as it had been experienced by generations before her. She may have been a short and small woman, but I'll bet she was tall in her saddle. She loved horses. Horses were greatly valued by her people. They were a sign of wealth. She witnessed the killing of her horses and the burning of her teepee. She and her people were taken to Fort Sill and kept in the stockade. Her belongings may have been destroyed, but never her spirit. The old way was taken away, but they found another way.

The early missionaries to come to Kiowa country had a harsh life on the prairie, but come they did. Gotebo, my tahlee's uncle, was one of the first Christian converts in the tribe. He composed the first Kiowa hymn. My tahlee and grandfather were charter members of the Rainy Mountain Baptist Church, founded over a hundred years ago. When they accepted Christianity, they accepted it wholeheartedly. Mornings were greeted with prayer and song. The last thing said at night after the story hour were prayers. Sundays were spent at the church. I mean all day. Transportation to the church for them was by wagon. Food was carried in the pots and pans, and the dishes and eating utensils were taken also.

There was a worship service in the morning and Sunday school after dinner. The evening service was held after Sunday school. Luke Toyebo shared this story about Tahlee with me. While the evening service was being held inside the church, she was outside with someone's baby on her back. She noticed that storm clouds were coming from the southwest. Kiowas have a healthy respect for storms. Out on that flat land you head for shelter from a storm. She became very uneasy and listened impatiently to the singing coming from the church. When the song finally came to an end and the people filed out she asked partly in Kiowa and partly in English why they were singing "lights are burning" when there was a storm coming? The story is funnier when told in Kiowa.

Atah was indeed an unusual woman. Her life and her example are uplifting to all who knew her. She gave love unconditionally, to me and to all the others. My younger sister, Gayle Roulain, remembers how Tahlee used to run her fingers over Gayle's face and she did the same to me to measure how much we had grown. She was a loving woman and it was demonstrated in her work, her beadwork, her cradles and in the way she lived her life. She never learned English. I was not very confident in speaking Kiowa, but we understood each other very well. I hear in my dreams the sound of her and Grandpa laughing. The Kiowa hymns are still being sung in the Kiowa churches. The daily prayers are still being offered to God by her grandchildren and their families. She has a great-grandson who is noted for his beadwork. She has great-great grandchildren and a great-great-great-grandchild who attend the church she helped to start. Her descendants are scattered from Washington State to Arizona, Colorado and Oklahoma. There are lawyers, a physician, educators, administrators, a nurse and many still in school. Christina Simmons, a nurse who worked on the White River Apache Reservation for many years, said there were many times in her work that she remembered her grandmother's spirit and that enabled her to fulfill her job. All of these people came from a woman who spoke no English but left the example of an indomitable spirit.

Atah and all of the other cradle makers of her day and those of today have one great feeling in common. That feeling is love. They were and are proud of their children, grandchildren, and all those yet to come. Atah was many things, but I am especially glad she was Tahlee, my grandmother.

NOTES

1. Delores Toyebo Harragarra is the daughter of Lewis Toyebo. Luke Toyebo, Peggy Toyebo Tsoodle, Patricia Toyebo Noel are the children of Milton Toyebo. Carolyn Hunt Lujan, Christina Hunt Simmons and Julia Hunt Geiogomah are the daughters of Ruth Mary Toyebo Hunt. Evelyn Toyebo Longhorn, Carlos Toyebo, Bernadine Toyebo Rhoades, Charles Leon Toyebo and Gayle Toyebo Roulain are the children of Charles Toyebo. The memories of Tahlee from some of these people, especially Carolyn Lujan and Christina Simmons, are what I am relating here.

2. Ioleta Hunt McElhaney was the first Kiowa woman minister. Her father was George Hunt, interpreter and tribal historian.

3. See Wilbur S. Nye, *Carbine and Lance,* 1937, p. 237 for further interpretation of this event. Atah served as informant to Nye.

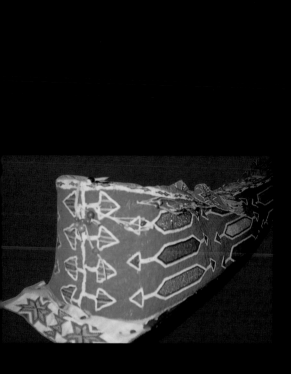

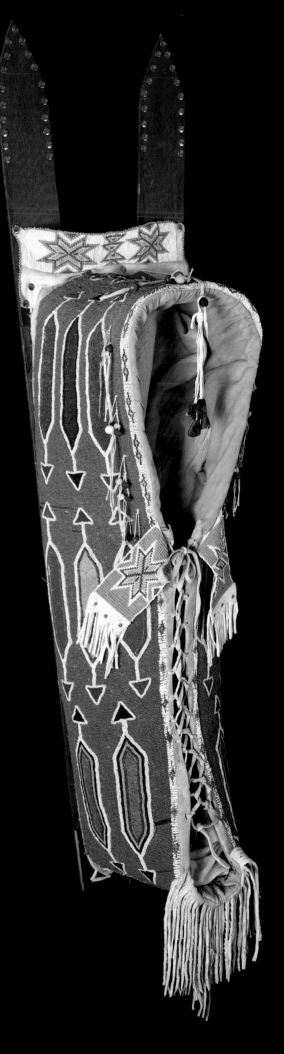

Fig. 7.1
Lattice cradle and detail, fully beaded, Kiowa, made by Millie Durgan Goombi (Saintohoodle) ca. 1909. L: 116 cm plus fringe. Wood, tacks, canvas, tanned deerskin, rawhide, glass beads, brass and steel beads, cotton cloth, cotton thread, sinew. Beadwork of elongated hexagons ending in triangles, designs and colors symmetrical on each side. Cover had been rolled up and removed from boards; later restored by maker's daughter and granddaughter by replacing lining, adding loom-woven tabs and bib, remounting on new boards. Private Collection. Photograph by Derek Jennings.

CHAPTER VII

Gifts of Love: Millie Durgan and a Family Artistic Tradition

by SHARRON AHTONE HARJO
(Saintohoodle, Killed with a Blunt Arrow)

SAINTOHOODLE, "Killed with a Blunt Arrow," is the Kiowa name of Millie Durgan Goombi (fig. 7.2). She was a white child who was captured in 1864 at the age of eighteen months by a Comanche-Kiowa raiding party in Youngs County, Texas. She was adopted by Gray Mare and Ahmate, and raised as a loved only child. She married into the respected warrior family, Goombi, and had many children. Her identity was known by few, for Millie chose to stay with the people she knew, the Kiowa (fig. 7.3).

For me, her life has been an identifying part of mine, for I, too, bear the name of Saintohoodle. Millie Durgan Goombi is my great-grandmother. She was my mother's grandmother and my grandmother's mother. My mother's name is Evelyn Tahome Ahtone and my grandmother's name was Almeta Jane Goombi. Millie Durgan is part of my life because of the family cultural ties of our Kiowa people. Each of us who are descendants of Millie Durgan know of her story and how she became a Kiowa.

My earliest recollection of the maternal side of my family were the photographs of Millie Durgan. These photographs hung high upon the east wall of my grandparent's bedroom. I recall sitting on the bed asking to be reassured that I understood the relationship of each person to the other. Under that same bed was a treasure of beads that were perhaps handed down to my grandmother from Millie Durgan. Maybe these were leftover beads from the hanks that are on the cradles she made. Perhaps the needles and thread are those used by Millie. I know there is a crossover artistic relationship between us.

I have always felt that the arts are an obligation for our people. Our cultural relationships are often centered on aesthetic values. They are a means of expressing love. We were taught to appreciate the art forms; they were in our houses; they were our toys; they were on the wall. The artists were family and friends as well as artists, like my great-grandmother Millie Durgan and my grandmother Tahdo, both cradle makers.

Fig. 7.2
Millie Durgan (Saintohoodle). Courtesy Jacob Ahtone Collection.

It is my understanding that Kiowa arts and crafts were created by specialists. All Kiowa children are special, from the firstborn to those that follow, and all are loved, and somehow the relationships create a need for a material object to show that love. The result, in earlier times, was a gift of love in the form of a beautifully beaded cradle. Cradles might be made by a grandmother or an auntie for a child in their family, or they might be commissioned by someone who would come to a specialist in cradle making and ask her to make a cradle for them. The cradles were often made for *auday* (special) children, usually a first-born grandchild. Auday children were favored with gifts and attention from within a family. The cradles were also available for those other people in a family who might wish to use them for their infants, since not every child was given a beaded cradle.

Through oral tradition we are able to connect our particular cradle maker, Millie Durgan, with her cradles. Photographs also document the use of the cradles within the Goombi family and its descendants (fig. 7.4). And our family cradles still exist as heirlooms. We have cherished the cradles to this day and take pride in knowing that our children will be photographed in these masterpieces.

Fig. 7.3
The Goombi family: (l to r) Ellen, Joe, Lillian, Goombi, Almeta Jane. Courtesy Museum of the Great Plains, Sam DeVenney Collection 265.

It is difficult for me to put into words the exact meaning of what Millie Durgan might have wanted to express in her work. I did not know her, as she passed away in 1934. What I can tell you are my observations – as an artist – of her work on cradles in comparison to the slightly later work on cradles made by my paternal grandmother, Tahdo. The method of construction was similar; the materials available were different, and they preferred different color combinations and designs. Millie Durgan used smaller size beads, some in metallic tones. She used basic geometric shapes such as circles, triangles, and elongated diamonds or hexagons and the overall work was symmetrical, with small design units. There was also some floral design. One recurring design in the patterns of Millie Durgan's cradles looks like arrow tips in succession. This may relate to her Indian name, Saintohoodle, "Killed with a Blunt Arrow."

Tahdo, in contrast, used large, simple, leaf or club-like shapes, with multiple outlines, in light colors on dark backgrounds, and almost always beaded narrow, geometric borders around her cradles. As did most Kiowa beadworkers, both women outlined their colorful shapes in contrasting white.

The Millie Durgan Goombi cradle in this exhibition was made for Henry Autoubo in 1909 (fig. 7.5). For some reason the cradle was taken apart. Parts of the original construction have since been discarded. The beautiful outer cover of beadwork was retained and stored away for a number of years. It is my understanding that the beadwork was to be thrown away, until rescued by my maternal grandmother, Almeta Jane Goombi Poolant. Many of the original beads were broken off. With diligence and care Grandma Jane put the cradle back together. There are new structural parts and embellishments of woven beadwork that are reflective of the time period of the early 1950s.

I remember the family members who gave so much of their talent that we children might share and be instilled with a cultural pride in the arts. Almeta Jane Goombi Poolant, the daughter of Millie Durgan, was as special as Kiowa grandmothers can be (fig. 7.6). It is hard to explain the nature of this relationship. Grandma Jane was tall, fair complexioned, with smiling green eyes that reflected a gentle being. As I had known for as far back as I remember, she looked much like the early pho-

Fig. 7.4
Millie Durgan made a cradle of netted beadwork for her granddaughter, Luti Augun Seta, shown here with her mother, Lillian Goombi Hunt, ca. 1912. Note the similarity in bead design of small repeated diamonds and netted stitch type between the tabs on Lillian Hunt's hide dress and the cradle. Courtesy Museum of the Western Prairie, Altus, Oklahoma.

tographs of Millie Durgan. Grandma Jane was known for her beadwork. She made moccasins, and purses, and I think her specialty was the medallions that are essential to Kiowa clothing. She carried over color schemes like that of her mother – primary and secondary colors outlined in contrasting white.

My relationship with my grandmother is so ingrained that there are days that I long to return to have those special moments with Grandma Jane. I recall she would awaken early, dip water from a bucket into the enamel wash basin for her morning ritual of

Fig. 7.5
Henry Autoubo (Ahtebone) in cradle made by Millie Durgan,
ca. 1909. Courtesy Museum of the Great Plains, Sam
DeVenney Collection 782.

cleansing her face and hands. From the water basin she would dampen her unbraided hair, and promptly make her way to a wooden chair next to the north window in the living area. There with her wire brush she would stroke her waist-length hair until it was readied to fashion into two long braids. These were wound about to form a flat oval at the nape of her neck, and clipped with two silverstone hair barrettes. All the while she would be singing Baptist church hymns like "Blessed Assurance," and "At the Cross."

Grandma Jane lived in the house that had belonged to Millie Durgan and, with the house, I am sure the routine was established. Grandma Jane's routine was set, each day making a great country breakfast which included plenty of strong coffee made in the enamel pot on the gas burner stove. After dishes, and morning chores of feeding chickens and gathering eggs, there was time to listen to the radio before having to cook lunch for Grandpa Steve who had been out at the old place to tend to farm chores. After lunch, you could be assured, as with most artists, it was time to get into the scheduled hours of beadwork.

One of my greatest memories was going into the bedroom where Grandma Jane had her beading materials. She would take out the materials she was working on to explain what she was going to do. Grandma Jane did not work on or at a table. On her lap in a flour sack of white muslin cloth would be her treasure of beads, needles, and thread, and whatever project she was doing. Her beadworking tasks included uninterrupted hours unless, of course, she had someone like me around who might just be inquisitive. There were times when by surprise she would make a beaded trinket, like a moccasin coin purse. My all-time favorite is a necklace made in peyote stitch of five tiny quail wishbones beaded in cutbeads. Grandma Jane was like that; there was always time for us and she was creative!

Although this essay is about cradles, I think it is important to acknowledge the distinctive relationships in Kiowa families. Grandma Jane made cradleboards in miniature for those who were lucky enough to receive one as a gift of love. Her sister-in-law, Maude Poolant Campbell, was another cradle maker. Her daughter Augustine Campbell Barse's photograph was taken as a baby in her own personal cradleboard. The cradle is part of the family heritage. Maude Campbell was known to have made several miniature cradleboards that remain in the possession of the original proud recipients. My older sister has one of the Maude Campbell creations as she is the first-born of the grandchildren. As tradition continues through the years, it can be said that the descendants of Millie Durgan have been entrusted to carry on her gifts of love. I am proud of the strong identity that carries forth within Kiowa generations through this art.

Fig. 7.6
Daughters of Millie Durgan – Almeta Jane Goombi
Poolant, with husband Steve Poolant, and Lillian
Goombi Hunt – American Indian Exposition, Anadarko,
Oklahoma, 1965. Courtesy Jacob Ahtone Collection.

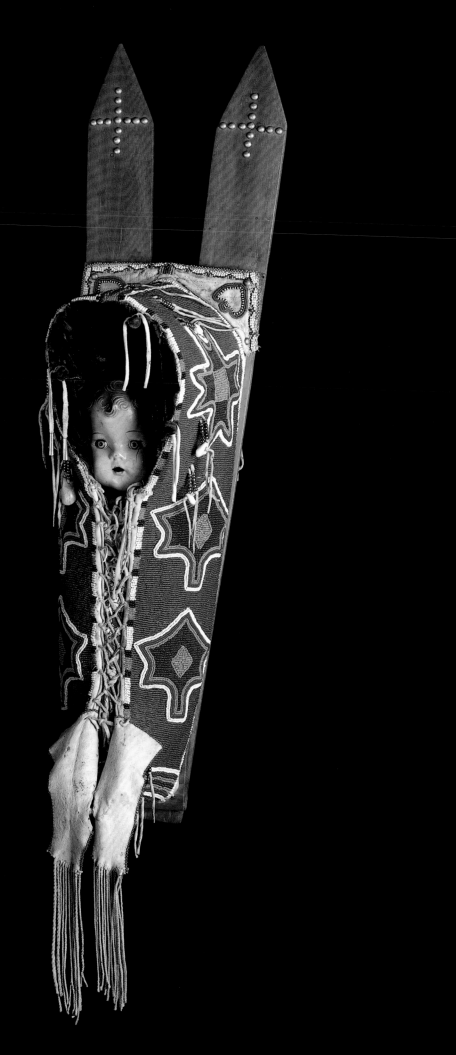

Fig. 8.1
Toy lattice cradle, fully beaded,
Kiowa, made by Tahdo (Tahgoy)
for a granddaughter ca. 1938. Her
husband Sam Ahtone carved the
boards. Commercial doll. L: 72 cm
plus fringe. Walnut boards, rawhide,
tanned deerskin, cotton cloth, fully
beaded with glass seed beads,
thread-sewn, in design of abstract
leaves, vertical layout on each side
of cover of two similar motifs, one
different motif; bead colors different, designs symmetrical on each
side of cover; geometric border
design. Private collection. Photograph by Derek Jennings.

CHAPTER VIII

I Remember How They Did That

by JACOB AHTONE

L ET ME INTRODUCE MYSELF. My name is Jacob Ahtone. I was given an Indian name, Atahhoaiie, by my grandfather. It means "Going to (Trailing) the Enemy." I was born February 28, 1918 to Samuel Ahtone and Tahdo (figs. 8.2, 8.3). My father was one of the first to be educated by non-Indians, having attended Carlisle Institute in Pennsylvania and Hampton Institute. He returned to Indian Territory and became involved with the American Baptist Home Mission Society and worked as an interpreter to the Kiowa Indians for the Rainy Mountain Kiowa Indian Baptist Church. The church was established in 1893 and is still operating.

Sam's paternal grandparents and his maternal grandpa were Mexican captives. The descendants of these captives all married into the Kiowa tribe. I primarily credit the religious background of Sam for contributing to his raising a stable family – or it may have been hybrid vigor from the mixture of Spanish and Kiowa blood.

My mother Tahdo (Medicine Sage), was a full-blood Indian, but with a small mixture of Absoluka (Crow) likely from the time when there was inter-marriage with the Crows while the two tribes occupied the Yellowstone Valley and the Big Horn Valley in Montana.

Tahdo's father's name was Zabile (Big Arrow). As a warrior he was wounded by a handgun shot over the shoulder of a fast departing mail carrier. The bullet entered his left eye and exited below his right ear. An old medicine man, Tay Bole, cleaned the wound and applied a poultice of prickly pear leaves to it and the wound rapidly healed. Zabile died in 1923, aged about 97 years.

My involvement with the cradles came about because my mother was a cradle maker. The museum

Fig. 8.2
Tahdo, "Old Lady Ahtone," (1879–1966). Courtesy Western History Collections, University of Oklahoma Library, SWOC 103.

Fig. 8.3
Tahdo and her husband, Sam Ahtone. Courtesy Mohawk
Trading Post, Clinton, Oklahoma.

invited my participation because I was somewhat familiar with the process of putting a Kiowa cradle together, having watched my mother design and make the cover and my father process the lattice framework.

The framework was made usually of hardwood that was indigenous to the area. In the days of my familiarity, these were bois d'arc (Osage orange), walnut, oak of various kinds, cedar, and ash. Some may have used such soft woods as pine or willow, but hardwoods were generally preferred.

In preparing the wood pieces, a hardwood of suitable length was selected. Preference was given to pieces with little or no knots as the wood had to be split with the grain to its approximate length, width, and thickness, and subsequently rubbed to a smooth finish.

In as much as the Kiowa cradleboard appears to be an item of fairly recent date I am not familiar with what primitive tools may have been used. My father used metal tools that he was able to find in early hardware stores or around blacksmith shops. There may have been times when he asked a blacksmith about tools or had him fashion a work tool. His wood-working tools included an ax, iron wedge (for splitting logs etc.), hatchet, machete, meat cleaver, butcher knife, draw knife, wood rasp, and later, carpenter's planes, including a small block plane.

Final touches to the wood pieces were usually accomplished by using a broken window pane as a scraper, after which sandpaper was used. I imagine stone – including sandstone – was used prior to the availability of sandpaper and steel wool.

When the boards were complete in size and design, I recall dad placing them a short distance from an open flame to heat them thoroughly. Following a satisfactory heating period to harden and darken the wood, he used animal fat to give it a pleasing sheen. Sometimes he heated the pieces several times until he was satisfied with the texture, color, and sheen.

The final size and shape of the boards I believe was determined after consultation with the maker of the cover. I am not aware that my father had a formula or equation to apply to the proportions of the framework. But I've never seen a finished cradle that appeared asymmetrical due to the cut of the boards. The sharpened end pieces always appeared to be at an angle of

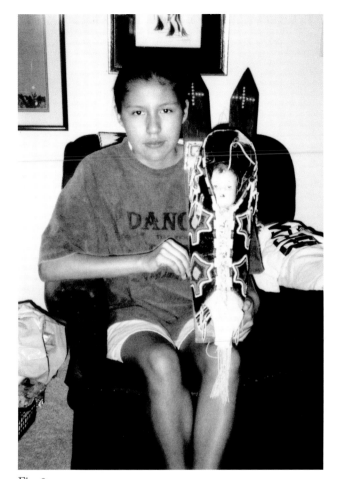

Fig. 8.4
Tahnee Ahtone Harjo, great-granddaughter of Tahdo, with cradle made by Tahdo. Toy cradles were made with the same care as full-sized ones. As children played, they learned how cradles were constructed. Photograph by Barbara Hail, 1995.

almost 60 degrees with the length of the two diagonal side cuts equal to the width of the board. The boards were fixed by lacing the buckskin thongs on to cross pieces. The distance between the boards and the angle at which they were placed was important. If the boards ran parallel to one another, the cradle appeared out of balance; or if the angle of run between the boards was too great, it too created an unbalanced appearance.

Holes for the lacing on the cross pieces and for lacing on the soft cover were originally burned through with sharpened, heated metal rods. Later, when tools could be purchased, a brace and bit were used and now, electric drills can be used. Before the electric drill, small holes were made by a small hand drill.

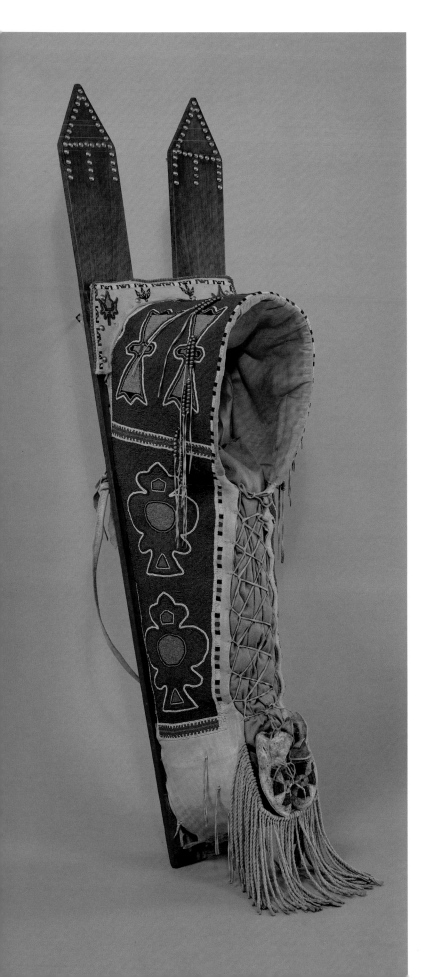

The placement of the holes for all lacing was prescribed by the maker of the cradle cover. My mother used nine holes, the lacing between them forming four squares, to secure each end of the cradle cover to the boards (fig. 8.6). There does not appear to be a common method of lacing the cross pieces or the soft cover. This I believe to be the personal preference of the cover designer.

My mother is reported to have made up to eight full size cradleboards and many toy cradles (figs. 8.1, 8.5). It is not known when she made her first cradle. The last full size cradles were made for William Tonepahote, a grandson born in 1930, and for grandson Vernon Ahtone, born in 1926. I had the privilege of seeing the work in progress, both on the cover and on the wood lattices.

Mother had no fixed work schedule, but she did work steadily and regularly on the projects. She worked five to seven hours per day and nearly every day. The Kiowas were forbidden by taboo to start a cradle for a baby until after the baby's birth and the cradle had to be made available prior to the baby's first birthday lest the child outgrow the cradle. Therefore, it is estimated that a cradle was completed in about ninety days.

The cradle making was not often a cooperative work between two or more people. For my mother, the project was a solo task except for my father's woodworking.

Tahdo did not place her work on a table. In the summer she sat on a knee-high platform that was about the width of a ¾ bed. She sat flat on the platform with her work and supplies spread within an arm's reach in

Fig. 8.5
Lattice cradle, Kiowa, probably made by Tahdo, 1915–1920. Attached baby moccasins in Cheyenne/Arapaho style, may have been later additions when cradle was for sale in the 1930s at Mohonk Lodge, Clinton, Oklahoma, close to Cheyenne and Arapaho communities. L:120.5 cm plus fringe. Wood, brass and nickel tacks, tanned deerskin, canvas, glass beads. Particular design and construction traits including bead designs of large, isolated, abstract leaf shapes with multiple raised outlining, borders in small, geometric designs, bib with leaf design, bead colors, and distinctive manner of securing cover to boards through nine hole lacing, points to Tahdo as the maker. Denver Art Museum, The L. D. and Ruth Bax Collection 1985.99.1

front of her. When at work she did not stop working when visitors came. She could talk to visitors and continue her beading or what ever else she was doing. Much of the time she was working, a daughter or granddaughter would be present to watch the progress of the work and hear stories of days gone by or receive instructions on how to live happily. As a son, I was privileged to visit and observe the techniques she used in completing projects.

Tahdo's supplies were bundled in either a diaper or dish cloth and included beading needles, thread, scissors, pen knife, awl, scraps of buckskin, and of course a considerable assortment of beads.

Tahdo used leaf motifs quite a bit. She took a natural leaf and simulated it by cutting a pattern on heavy brown paper – usually a grocery bag. If the pattern was not satisfactory she made new cuts until she obtained one she liked. Upon getting an acceptable pattern she drew it with pencil on the material she was using for a base. After "marking" the outline for the design she beaded over the pencil marks and subsequently filled in the interior of the design. The beauty of her beading craft was not only in affixing the beads but also in choosing colors that were both compatible and coordinated and pleasing to see. In open areas of the design she applied the so-called lazy stitch.

After the cover was fully beaded, Tahdo proceeded to attach it to the lattice boards lacing through the boards from the back after which she put in a lining of broad cloth or satin. She finished the cradle by beading the borders – called edge work.

Cradles were finished and decorated in a variety of ways. Some had hand-rolled fringes as tassels at the foot end of the cradle; some had loose flaps of buckskin or some other way to cover the joining of the cover-halves. The covers generally were two pieces beaded separately and put together when beading was complete.

The oak leaf design, so common as a motif on many Kiowa articles of dress, I feel to be an outgrowth of winning designs on artifacts exhibited by Tahdo in the early Indian Days of Albuquerque, New Mexico. A field matron of the Bureau of Indian Affairs by the name of Suzie Peters used to assemble Kiowa art and artifacts for shows at Albuquerque. Annually the Kiowa Exhibit won First Prize. Tahdo and Maggie Smoky were the

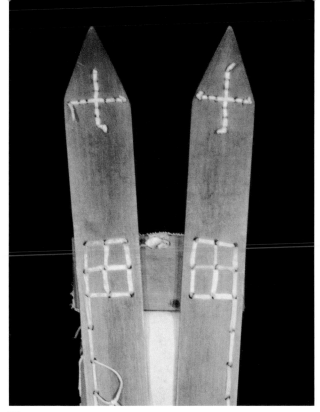

Fig. 8.6
Tahdo laced her cradle cover to the boards in a distinctive manner, securing it through nine holes at each end. This detail is of a cradle now in the Museum of the Great Plains, made by Tahdo for grandson William Tonepahote in 1930. Photograph by Rip Gerry.

major beadworkers for the Kiowa Exhibit. Because the Exhibit was considered outstanding and truly representative of Kiowa art many people started to use the oak leaf on their craft work. Therefore, it could be said that Tahdo was one of the first innovators to use and have the oak leaf, considered as representative art of the Kiowa. Today there is much use of the oak leaf in Kiowa beaded articles.

Sam Ahtone and Tahdo made a good team in the making of Kiowa cradleboards. Individuals and museums who have possession of these cradles have items that represent the talent and love that went into their making.

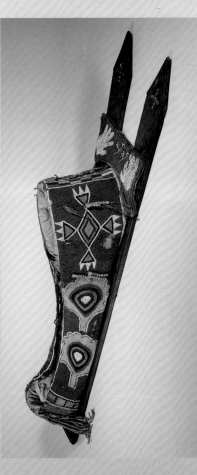

Fig. 9.1
Lattice cradle, both sides, and
detail of top of cover, Kiowa, made
by Keintaddle and Paukeigope
before 1898 for Paukeigope's first son,
Stephen Mopope. L: 108.5 cm plus
fringe. Boards are hand-hewn Osage
orange (bois d'arc). Cover sides asymmetric in bead design and color.
According to descendant Vanessa
Paukeigope Jennings, the beaded
hands in the bib honor a war deed
of Ghoulayee, Stephen Mopope's
paternal grandfather, who counted
coup on a Spanish officer. In trying
to take the officer's red cape from
him, he pushed away his face with
hands that were bloody from battle.
Colorado Springs Fine Arts Center,
Debutante Ball Committee Purchase
in memory of Vesta Tutt, TM 1986.7.
See also figs. 9.5, 10.5.

CHAPTER IX

Keintaddle

by BERNADINE HERWONA TOYEBO
RHOADES *(Tosahnhaw, Coming Home)*

KEINTADDLE was born in 1849 and died August 23, 1938 at the age of 89 years (fig. 9.2). Her husband was Gatikaunmah (They Call Him Warrior). They had three sons and three daughters. The sons, Daubein, Saquodlequoie and Ketitagope preceded her in death. Her daughters were Tahkeihoodle, Paugeigope and Padoti. Their married names in English are Martha Ware, Etta Mopope and Magdalene Paddlety.

Keintaddle's only living grandchildren at the present time are Estelle Turkey, daughter of Saquodlequoie, David Leroy Paddlety, son of Magdalene and David Paddlety, and Daniel Ware, son of Martha Ware.

Donepi is recorded at the Bureau of Indian Affairs as Keintaddle's father and Sapoodle as her mother. Donepi had another name, Pautaudletay (Poor Buffalo), and this was the name Keintaddle used for her father.

Keintaddle was my "big sister" (my great-grandmother). The "Kiowa way" of acknowledging kinship can seem confusing but is really simple. Your mother's sisters are called "mother" and her brothers are your uncles. Your father's brothers are addressed as "father" and his sisters are your aunts. The children (your cousins) are your brothers and sisters. Their children then become yours and the cycle of kinship begins anew. Great-grandparents are called "big brothers" or "big sisters" and the great-grandchildren are called "little brothers" or "little sisters." As a result of such kinship, we have grandmothers and grandfathers, brothers, sisters, aunts, uncles and children throughout Kiowa land. When we attend Kiowa functions, it is a great feeling to greet all our kinsmen and know there is love and caring all around. It has become a challenge for our children to find someone who is not a relative. Keintaddle had brothers, and half-brothers/sisters and their respective families, thereby increasing the number of relatives we have in Kiowa land. I love that feeling of connection with her that this kinship still provides (fig. 9.3).

My great-grandmother Keintaddle lived near the Washita River west of Anadarko, Oklahoma. The area has a lot of red sandstone, and so it is known as Red

Fig. 9.2
Keintaddle 1935. Courtesy Smithsonian Institution 88-733.

Stone. This is where she raised her family and it is the area where I grew up.

My mother, Alice Poorman Paddlety Toyebo, was a granddaughter of Keintaddle and the daughter of Magdalene Paddlety. Mother was the eldest of twelve children so Keintaddle took my mother to bring up in her household. This was not unusual. It happened a lot and still does today. The whole family lived very close to one another at Red Stone, so Keintaddle's house was never far from any of her children. My mother knew

her own genealogy and everyone else's because of her grandmother. She always said, "That's what my grandma told me" when she told us anything of the past.

Keintaddle was a well-known beadworker widely recognized for her talent. My grandmother, Magdalene, and her sister Etta Mopope (also my grandma) became beadworkers (fig. 9.4). Keintaddle had granddaughters, great-granddaughters and great-great-granddaughters who have taken up the same kind of work.

Estelle Turkey, a granddaughter of Keintaddle, still lives in the area. She said her father, Saquodlequoie, loved his mother very much. They lived next to Keintaddle's house in a teepee. Estelle, who is now 87, remembers her grandmother well and how industrious she was. In a nice long visit not long ago, Estelle told me the following:

> We lived there at Red Stone. My dad and his blind brother (Daubein) lived with their mother. All of her children were born there. The home place is located near the Red Stone Baptist Church. It had big trees which shaded the house so no arbor was needed. She made moccasins for men and women. She made leggings. She was well known for her beadwork. I was young and did not observe her so closely. My grandmother worked inside the house and the children played outside. You know how children are – they don't pay attention. My grandmother was industrious. She made buckskin costumes for men, women and children. She made baby cradles for family and for people who came to her to

Fig. 9.3
Four generations of artists, ca. 1898. L to r: Sapoodle (mother of Keintaddle), Paukeigope, who holds her infant son Stephen Mopope, and Keintaddle. Courtesy Western History Collections, University of Oklahoma Library, Phillips 96a.

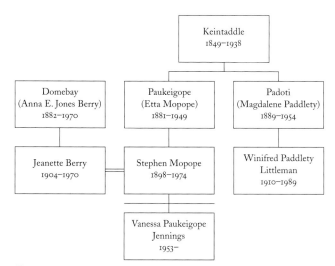

Fig. 9.4
Chart of a Cradle-making Family. All of these women were cradle makers. Stephen Mopope was an artist. Beadworking skills were passed down and shared along kinship lines.

have her make cradles for them. Not everybody made
those kind of cradles. Certain ones knew how to make
them the old time way from a long time ago. She was one
of them. She got her beads from some of the northern
tribes, probably the Cheyenne and Arapaho. She made
hides, put them on the ground on top of canvas, and
staked them down. Grandma did that and so did her
husband. She was also paid for some of her work. She
was paid in coins that were yellow, maybe it was gold
coins. They would be given to her sometimes in bags.[1]

Estelle tells of her grandparents owning several
kinds of horses – riding horses and horses that pulled
the wagons and buggies. Keintaddle had a wagon and a
buggy. They went often to Anadarko to purchase their
groceries. She sold some of her beadwork to the people
in town.

Keintaddle was the center of life in the Red Stone
community. She donated the land where the Red Stone
Baptist Church parsonage is located. The church itself
is on land donated by one of her brothers. Her son-in-
law, David Paddlety, my grandfather, was a preacher
there (fig. 9.5). Keintaddle's daughter, Magdalene, was
my grandmother. Three of her grandsons, Stecker,
Victor, and David Leroy Paddlety became pastors there
following in the footsteps of their father. Many family
members still reside in the community.

Winifred Littleman, daughter of Magdalene, was a
well-known beadworker in her own right. She was a
cradle maker also, and though she is no longer with us,
her talent lives on (figs. 9.6, 9.7).

Keintaddle was an *auday mata'un*, which translates
as a very special girl. Her father, Pautaudletay, was a
great warrior and a member of the TonKonGaw (Black
Legging) Warrior Society. Keintaddle was a princess –
known as *auday mata'un* – of this society. *Auday mata'un*
in this context is a title; otherwise, it is used to describe
a very special girl.

Keintaddle was born during a time of great change
for the Kiowa people, when many battles were fought to
retain their way of life. Keintaddle's father was involved
in perhaps the final one in Palo Duro Canyon. This spec-
tacular canyon, long a refuge for Kiowas, is south of
Amarillo in the panhandle of Texas. In 1874 it was used
by the Kiowas, Comanches and Cheyennes as a refuge
from the weather and from the United States troops.
On September 28, 1874, Colonel Ranald Mackenzie

Fig. 9.5
Padoti (Magdalene Paddlety) (1889–1954) and a baby in a
cradleboard made by Padoti's mother Keintaddle and sister
Paukeigope (seated, l). Padoti's husband David Paddlety
(1880–1939) stands. This cabinet card from the Russell Studio,
Anadarko, was sewn to a cardboard Christmas greeting bearing
the message, "Merry Christmas, blessings still be thine."
Courtesy Yancy Littleman Collection.

attacked the canyon encampments of these three tribes.
He destroyed the teepees, captured and later destroyed
1000 of their horses, and drove the Indians out of the
canyon. Pautaudletay was one of those Indians, and
Keintaddle told of this incident many times to my
mother.[2]

The story according to my mother is that the
Kiowas were in a deep canyon hiding from the U.S.
Army, when their encampment was surprised. Only
two trails led into the canyon, one on the south and one
on the north. The soldiers had to come down single file
through the north entrance; they surprised the Kiowas
and the other tribes that were down in the canyon.

Fig. 9.6
Winifred Paddlety Littleman and her husband Milburn Steve
Littleman, Sr., 1960s. Courtesy Yancy Littleman Collection.

Pautaudletay and his group went up the south trail to
escape. He was wounded so he directed his people to
put him down behind a rock so that he could hold off
the pursuing soldiers with his rifle. He was able to give
the escapees some time and managed to escape himself.
He had many wives as was the custom and one of his
children was a young boy who was crippled. He said
that this son was one of the main reasons he fought so
hard to escape: "What would happen to the poor boy,
who would take care of him if I couldn't make it?"

He lived to tell the story and Keintaddle would tell
this story to my mother and would teach her the song
he sang as he held off the soldiers. Family history has
passed this story on by word of mouth because Kiowas
have no written language. Keintaddle passed on her
stories to her grandchildren. My mother, who lived
with her, remembered many of the stories told to her.
One of the great duties of being a grandmother was to
tell the stories of old. The story of Pautaudletay is one
that has been shared by my mother many times.

Due to the modern conveniences of today, we have
some stories on audio tape. My mother recorded for me
a song she said her grandmother Keintaddle sang to my
sister, Evelyn Longhorn. The translation of the words is
as follows: "the little girl was dancing and she wanted
the other little girls to dance with her but they did not
want to because she had a ragged dress on and she didn't
have any shoe strings on her shoes and every time she

Fig. 9.7
Lattice cradle, Kiowa, made by Winifred Paddlety Littleman
for her first grandson, Yancy, in 1963. L: 98 cm. Boards short,
colored with magic marker. Partially beaded in abstract floral,
leaf, geometric designs, in vertical layout of two similar motifs
and one different motif, symmetrical on each side, in overlay
stitch on black velvet over canvas; blue cotton lining; bib; hide
fringing, lacing. Yancy Littleman Collection. Photograph by
Sandy Settle.

would get up to dance her shoes would fall off, so she told the other little girls to dance without shoes because she couldn't keep hers on. Because she had a *bo-ohn* mother who could not keep her properly dressed." *Bo-ohn*, translated, means one who is inept and cannot do things properly. It is a cute song and I can almost see the expression on the face of the singer. It shows much affection for the little one, just as the making of a cradle or the wrapping of the baby and singing a lullaby to put the little one to sleep shows the love and care the old ones had for children.

Keintaddle, like all the others of her day, had to experience a complete change in the way she lived. In reading the history of this period, it is amazing to me that these people survived the turbulent times with their spirit so strong and were able to pass this spirit on to their descendants. Keintaddle lived through the measles and smallpox epidemics, and the change from a nomadic life on the prairie, moving from one hunting area to another following game, to one of living in a house

under a big tree. I was seven years old when she died. I was too young to realize what was lost to us. My mother, fortunately for us, passed on some of Keintaddle's tales of the past. Keintaddle passed on many of her stories to Estelle Turkey and to David Leroy Paddlety and we are glad they are here to share them with us.

These stories leave a picture in my mind of Keintaddle and her people of industriousness, wisdom, wit, humor, talent, and a great love for family. That love is shown in her handiwork. She passed on her talent in beadworking to her daughters, grandchildren, great-grandchildren, great-great-grandchildren and perhaps it will continue on through future generations. The Kiowas thought of their descendants' welfare and well-being. They spoke of their future generations and put down a path for them to follow through their songs, dances, love of God, and their creativity. Keintaddle's grandson, David Leroy Paddlety, teaches Kiowa language classes in Anadarko, Oklahoma. Vanessa Jennings, a great-great-granddaughter teaches beadwork, moccasin-making and the making of leggings, buckskin dresses and most importantly, the making of cradles.

In doing the research for this small window into the past, one thing leaps out at me and that is the love of family the Kiowas had, the way they thought of their cousins, aunts, uncles, grandparents, and great-grandparents. Despite the present day technology we enjoy, the life they lived on the prairie, even with its difficulties and hardships, must have been exciting. When I see the work they did so many years ago, gratitude fills me because I know it is with love that they made their works of art. They took pride in doing their tasks well. That is the Kiowa way. That is love.

Fig. 9.8
Keintaddle carrying her grandson Stephen ca. 1900.
Courtesy Vanessa Paukeigope Jennings Collection.

NOTES

1. Estelle Turkey, interview with author, 1997.
2. For the U.S. Army's version of this action see Wilbur S. Nye, *Carbine and Lance,* pp. 221–225, Norman: 1937.

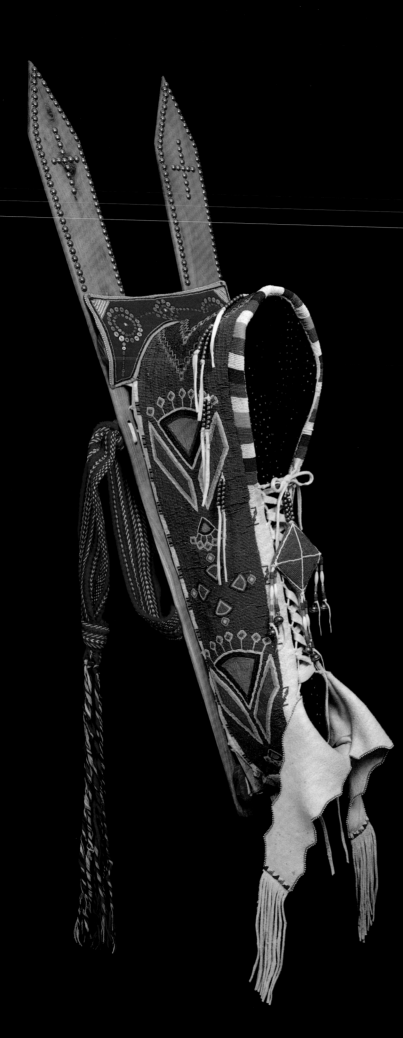

Fig. 10.1
Lattice cradle, both sides, Kiowa, made by Vanessa Paukeigope Jennings in 1998. L:113 cm plus fringe. Bois d'arc boards, tack-decorated; glass seed beads, brass beads, bone beads, canvas, tanned deerskin, wool broadcloth, sequins; beaded amulet. The cradle was dedicated to her sister Stevette, who died shortly after it was completed. Stevette was a favorite of their great-grandmother Anna E. Jones Berry, whose designs are used on the cradle. The variegated orange-red beads and greasy yellow beads had belonged to their grandmother Jeanette Berry, and the lavender beads to great-grandmothers Paukeigope and Keintaddle. Carl Jennings carved the boards and made the framework of rawhide and wood. Haffenreffer Museum of Anthropology, Brown University 98-18-1. Photograph by Cathy Carver.

CHAPTER X

Why I Make Cradles

by VANESSA PAUKEIGOPE JENNINGS

M Y NAME IS Vanessa Paukeigope Jennings. I am the oldest granddaughter of Stephen Mopope and Jeanette Berry. My grandparents raised me in an area of southwest Oklahoma known to other Kiowas as Red Stone. I continue to live on the Indian allotment where my grandparents had their home. When my time ends I plan to be buried there. As a child, every day of my life was saturated with songs, dancing, beadwork, prayers, laughter, stories, smiles and love. Today I try to continue that tradition with my own family. I started beading when I was eleven years old. One lesson that has stayed with me all these years is in words of my grandmother Jeanette: "No one lives forever. Pay attention because you are the one who will take my place!"… Now I understand that she was teaching me a culture that would form the foundation of my life. I understand now that culture is a conscious, consistent, deliberate passing on of knowledge taught every day by an older generation to the next generation. Her instructions were always prefaced with the words, "You tell your grandchildren that it's done this way because that's how my grandmother showed me!"

The admiration that I feel toward my ancestors is difficult to put into words. Jeanette Berry Mopope, my maternal grandmother, was Kiowa Apache. She was a singer, dancer, excellent beadworker and cradleboard maker. Jeanette's mother, Anna E. Jones Berry, was a Kiowa beadworker and cradleboard maker (figs. 10.3, 10.4). My maternal grandfather's mother was Paukeigope (Etta Mopope). She and her mother, Keintaddle, were prominent Kiowa women and active cradle makers, as well as beadworkers, singers, storytellers and knowledgeable informants for ethnologists, particularly for the Santa Fe Field School in 1935. My grandmother

and her mother-in-law Paukeigope beaded together in the living room or under a willow arbor. They wore traditional clothing of cloth dresses, braided hair, leather concho belts and moccasins or leggings until the last day of their lives on this earth.

Fig 10.2
Vanessa Paukeigope Jennings in 1999 with grandson Cade in broadcloth cradle she made for him. Courtesy Vanessa Paukeigope Jennings Collection.

Fig. 10.3
Vanessa as a child on the lap of her grandmother Jeanette Berry Mopope. Her great-grandparents, Tennyson and Anna E. Jones Berry, are seated next to them. Courtesy Vanessa Paukeigope Jennings Collection.

My primary instructor and the greatest influence in my life was Jeanette Berry Mopope. She always gave credit for her knowledge to her mother and to her mother-in-law, Paukeigope, for whom I am named (fig. 10.5). So, the technique that I use for the making of the cradleboard is a unique combination of information derived from these three women. I have the greatest respect for their extensive knowledge in making such a large variety of work – cradleboards, saddles, lances, moccasins, dresses, women's leggings, handbags and many other items necessary for a traditional life.

One aspect of my grandmother's teaching included a stern lecture on designs and color choices. She taught me to have respect for designs and to use only designs that belong to your family. These designs have a life and a history. It is disrespectful to "copy" another beadworker's design. Grandmother instructed me never to use designs that did not belong to me, "because I didn't raise a thief."

The only time that I could use another family's designs was if they were "given" to me by a family member. This has happened on several occasions. In one instance, the woman was an older beadworker and in poor health. She felt that by giving these designs to me, they would be safe until one of her children or grandchildren had an interest in beadworking. This represents both an honor and a burden for me. My friends have a serious concern, because they see me as a responsible and honorable person who will do what the family instructed, but such a responsibility causes fear in me, for what if their girls never develop an interest in beadworking?

I live in an area where many Indians do not really care about our traditional clothing or culture. They did not have the advantage of Jeanette Mopope's diligence. It was at Grandma Jeanette's insistence that I learned how to do beadwork and it is to her credit that I am able to do a wide variety of work. Anadarko and the surrounding communities in southwest Oklahoma are an economically depressed area. Today the small amount of tourist dollars forces many beadworkers to specialize in making only beaded rosettes, keychains, and earrings. This is what sells and keeps the bills paid.

Grandma Jeanette, Anna Jones, Paukeigope and Keintaddle insisted on teaching traditional arts and values in spite of governmental repression. Our traditional culture can not live without these values or its arts because they are connected. I will never separate myself from my culture because I am pledged to it through prayers. Grandma Jeanette explained that "Our prayers are what brought you here." If I walked away from my present life, I would have to walk away from those prayers and pledges and then who would I be?

In September, 1996 at the Plains Indian Seminar in Cody, Wyoming, I had a memorable experience. Dr. JoAllyn Archambault of the Smithsonian Institution gave the keynote address that opened the seminar by describing and discussing my art work. My husband Carl and I drove from Oklahoma to attend. Barbara Hail from the Haffenreffer Museum at Brown University, Rhode Island, asked me to help her give a presentation on Kiowa cradleboards. Barbara spoke about

the origin and history of Southern Plains cradleboards while I spoke on the methods I use to recreate Kiowa cradleboards today.

I had made a fully beaded Kiowa cradle based on my interpretation of one that my grandfather, Stephen Mopope, had been carried in. I used an old black and white photo that showed my grandfather peeking out of the cradle looking at the cameraman while Paukeigope, his mother, proudly carried him on her back. This single photograph that hangs on our wall at home was the only thing that remained in my family to document the joy of Stephen Mopope's earthly arrival (fig. 10.5). Keintaddle had made the cradleboard for my grandfather with the assistance of her daughter Paukeigope. Stephen was Keintaddle's oldest grandson so the two had a strong and loving relationship that my grandfather always spoke of with great affection.

Fig. 10.4
Anna E. Jones Berry, great-grandmother, and Jeanette Berry Mopope (in white buckskin dress), grandmother of Vanessa Paukeigope Jennings, ca. 1920. Courtesy Vanessa Paukeigope Jennings Collection.

Fig. 10.5
Paukeigope (Etta Mopope) carrying her baby Stephen Mopope
in the cradleboard she and her mother Keintaddle made.
Courtesy Museum of the Great Plains, Sam DeVenney
Collection 754. See fig. 9.1.

I wanted to make something that would honor my
grandfather and our family so I selected this idea. The
original cradle had disappeared and no one knew when
it left the family or could describe the circumstances of
its disappearance.

Imagine my surprise when Barbara Hail discovered the missing cradleboard as part of the collection of
the Taylor Museum, Colorado Springs Fine Arts Center
(see fig. 9.1). Our black and white photograph had reversed
the values of the light and dark colors and the detail was
difficult to make out. However, the final effect in my
finished cradleboard is one that I hope would have made
Keintaddle and Jeanette Mopope proud. The cradle is

now part of the Buffalo Bill Historical Center collection in Cody, Wyoming.

After viewing the Stephen Mopope cradle, I was
impressed by the beaded hands on the bib that covers
the top of the cradle. This design continues a tradition of
honoring Ghoulayee, Stephen Mopope's grandfather,
and his war deed of capturing a cape from a Mexican
officer after pushing in his face with his battle-bloodied
hands. Ghoulayee is remembered by both the Kiowa
Black Leggings Society and the family-based Ghoulayee
Descendants' Organization in their spring and fall cer-
emonials. Society members sing his song and wear red
capes in honor of his war deeds. By so doing they reinforce the fact that each of us has a history, and that it is
important to remember where you come from and why
you are here.

After the free days, the buffalo were gone and the
fruitful life of the past did not exist. The Kiowa were
brought to Anadarko and the surrounding areas as a
captive nation. They were forced to depend on Indian
Agents and the Government for food rations, annuity
payments and other kinds of support. It was a time of
deprivation and hardship. However, a woman had to be
strong. I am not speaking of physical strength but of
the emotional strength needed to overcome hardships
through courage, persistence and tenacity, and to battle
against the dominant culture of the Whites. If a woman
were weak, then the whole family was in danger of being
wiped out. A cradleboard represents to me that bare,
primitive essence of love that exists between a mother
and her newborn.

The missionaries, the army and the Indian Agents
were opposed to any form of traditional culture, such as
dancing and singing. The Kiowa were expected to assim-
ilate. My family continued their dancing, singing, and
prayer in secret, through the O-Ho-Mah Lodge Society.
My great-grandfather George Mopope was called into
the Agency at Anadarko and told that if he persisted in
these traditional practices his family's annuities and
rations would be withdrawn. George Mopope refused
and stated flatly that he would die before renouncing
his pledge to O-Ho-Mah (fig. 10.6).

His wife, Paukeigope, and her mother, Keintaddle,
nurtured the same love for tradition and it continued in
Paukeigope's son, Stephen Mopope, and his family.

Paukeigope and Keintaddle knew what it was to sacrifice and go hungry in order to save their children. They knew what agony it was to bury their beautiful babies. The hardships that they and so many other women endured to provide a way for someone like me fills my heart with pride. Stephen Mopope's marriage to Jeanette Berry was a continuation of that love for tradition and culture, and I, brought up by them, received their values. The strength of my grandmother looms over me every day of my life. I am only a shadow compared to my grandmother. I will always stand in awe of her!

Together they strengthened and beautified our lives through remembering the past: with stories of how Poor Buffalo encouraged the other warriors while they made a last stand at the Palo Duro Canyon, how as a child Maggie Smoky, later a noted cradleboard

Fig. 10.6
George and Etta Mopope (Paukeigope), 1901. Courtesy Western History Collections, University of Oklahoma Library, Phillips 14.

maker and beadworker, was rescued after falling from a galloping stallion by a female relative who leaned from a saddle and lifted the little girl up from the ground, and stories of how children were dressed in their best because their mothers believed the soldiers would kill them at the bottom of the canyon. I was always impressed by the incredible feats of courage in stories of the old times, such as the old grandfather who in 1833 rescued his infant grandchild by placing the carrying strap of the cradleboard in his mouth while he loosed arrows at the enemy Osage. This is the year the Kiowas called "The Year They Cut Off Our Heads."

THE CRADLES

In the late nineteenth century cradles were often beaded with large, complex, abstract, floral and geometric design elements. Those of the twentieth century continued these patterns and a few added the use of representational designs such as flags, buffalo, elk, deer, horses and other animals, human figures, and stars. I make cradles according to the traditional methods of the Kiowa and Kiowa-Apache, who are known for favoring bilateral asymmetry, often using different colors or designs on each side of a cradleboard. The imaginative use of color is what makes each cradle come alive! My personal favorites are the cradles that are partially beaded on red wool broadcloth. Now that a company makes broadcloth in eight different colors, it is my goal to make a cradle in each color.

In the free days and during the reservation period, the wood used for the boards was primarily bois d'arc or Osage orange. It is a hard wood that was found in great abundance and was also a favorite for bows for the men. Other hardwoods such as hickory, pecan, and maple were often used as well. Our people were adaptive; wood was salvaged from old cabinets and shipping crates to use for the cradles. My grandmother did this quite often and in 1954 she even stepped in to a small shop to purchase linoleum to use as a stiffener in the head and foot of the cradleboard that she was making for my sister Stevette! This came about because the price of a raw hide was too expensive, and my grandmother was not about to give her money to a shopkeeper who escalated his price because he believed that she could not buy what she needed elsewhere. I now

Fig. 10.7
"Mother and child," watercolor by Stephen Mopope, Kiowa, 1931. L: 28 cm x W: 20 cm. Courtesy Vanessa Paukeigope Jennings Collection.

have a precious cradle that is handmade by my grandmother. It is a silent testimony both to her artistic talents and to the strength of her character.

The color, design and artistry of cradleboards impress me as a celebration of life. These cradleboards are symbols of humanity honoring our unnamed sisters and grandmothers who rose up against overwhelming odds of wars, cultural genocide, death and other monumental events to celebrate a newborn's life as only women can: to represent a promise of hope for the future. In my work, I try to represent a continuation of culture from one generation to the next. I know the pain of losing a newborn as my sister, Stevette, experienced when her son Baldwin died shortly after birth. I had no words of comfort to voice, but my daughter and I stayed up all night to make a cradle and moccasins so that my nephew could make his journey along the Milky Way dressed in his best, in keeping with our traditions.

It is difficult to live this life that I have chosen. I have been told that it would be more profitable if I made the smaller, less expensive beaded items that could be sold quickly. I remember taking a blue, fully beaded cradleboard, a painted buffalo robe and beaded women's leggings to two different Indian stores in Anadarko, Oklahoma and to a shop on the Plaza in Santa Fe, New Mexico to sell. The opinion of each shop representative was that my work was too ethnic and would not sell. I make the cradles because no one else among my Kiowa and Apache people is interested. I am a stubborn woman and I do not want that knowledge to be lost. Long ago, my Grandma Jeanette told me, "When you see something that needs to be done, get up and take care of it. Don't be lazy or wait to be asked." I want to make sure that my grandmother's efforts are not lost. It is reassuring when I think that some of my life's goal is preserved in museums and I hope that my own children and grandchildren will come there one day looking for me and for my grandmother's instructions.

I once listened to an old recording of my grandmother and Paukeigope singing together. My grandmother said these songs would give us great comfort. They were recorded because she wanted to protect them from being lost. Her voice speaks to me across the years and touches me to this day. I heard her say, "Some day one of our own will come looking for us and we will be here waiting for them." Her love and concern reached toward unborn generations. Such traditional women live on through their influence on each of us and through memories of their prayers and art.

I have mentioned the Kiowa Apache because ethnologists, folklorists, and anthropologists have documented little of their culture. There are no active Kiowa Apache cradleboard makers living, although I know of several beautiful examples of their cradles in museums. Out of respect for my Kiowa Apache descent, it is necessary for me to recognize their contribution. If I did not acknowledge my Kiowa Apache lineage, I would be ignoring my grandmother, Jeanette Berry Mopope, my daughter, and my granddaughters Alex and Miss Elizabeth Morgan, who are enrolled with the Apache Tribe of Oklahoma. With the creation of each new piece that I make I think of my beautiful children, Gabriel Pokeitay Morgan, Seth Mopope Morgan and Summer Tsotkeigope Morgan.

> To my sons and daughter…
>
> Everything has a time…a beginning, a middle, and an end.
> Your time is beginning now…fresh, young and strong!
> Your way has been made through our prayers.
> Remember us.
> You are taking our place. Live a good life and enjoy it.
> Make us proud!

These words were spoken to me long ago by my grandmother Jeanette Berry Mopope at the old Mopope homeplace in Red Stone, where I still live, and I pass them on to my children. Our ways have traveled a long road. After my journey ends, my children will carry on these prayers and traditions. On our hill west of Red Stone there is always a pot of coffee on and plenty of time to visit. Please stop in and we can talk.

Fig. 10.8
Alex and Elizabeth Morgan (in cradle made by her grandmother), grandchildren of Vanessa Paukeigope Jennings. Courtesy Vanessa Paukeigope Jennings Collection.

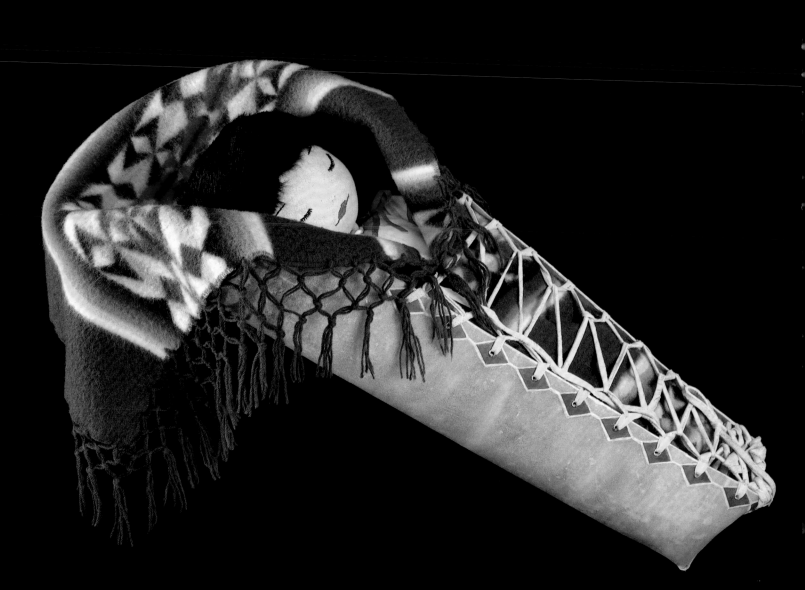

Fig. 11.1
Cradle *(haabikuno*, a lying down or
night cradle), with hide doll, Comanche,
made by Weckeah Parker in 1998.
L: 74 cm. Rawhide, paint; smoked,
brain-tanned deerskin; wool, glass
beads, silver, artificial fur. This cradle
is used for infants up to about four
months old. Haffenreffer Museum of
Anthropology, Brown University
98-27-1. Photograph by Cathy Carver.

CHAPTER XI

I Learned from my Elders

by WECKEAH *(Loping Along Searching)*

I GREW UP IN THE 1920S in a Comanche Indian Mission Camp located north of Lawton, Oklahoma and south of the local military base, Fort Sill. My parents were Musitah (Ed Clark) and Putsi, both original Comanche allottees, having received land from the U. S. Government in accordance with the Jerome Agreement of 1892. I presently live on my inherited Comanche allotment. I am enrolled ⁴/₄ Comanche (fig. 11.2). My mother's parents were Quanah Parker and his first wife Weckeah (fig. 11.4). They had five daughters, Nahmaku, Wuyuri, Wunuru, Putsi, and Tupusiup (figs. 11.5, 11.6). Quanah's parents were Putaku Nookoni and Cynthia Ann Parker. Weckeah's father was Wura Tsukupu. My father Musitah's parents were Nakitua (E.L. Clark) and Wumakoni. Wumakoni's father was Mahksuah. My grandmother Weckeah gave me her name.

Most of the people at the mission at that time spoke only Comanche. English was rarely heard except from the missionaries. I have sweet memories of my *kaku* (maternal grandmother) carrying me cozy and safe on her back snug in her *uhu* (blanket). Two of my maternal aunts with no children of their own helped with my parents' ten children. My grandmother Weckeah and my aunt Tupusiup loved and cared for me. My parents also gave loving attention to all their children. As is the Comanche way we call all our aunts *pia* (mother.).

My kaku, pia and I were often in our own camp dwelling. We slept on our *norunapu* (bed) on the ground. I remember it being very comfortable. When the weather began to get cold my kaku and pia would build a *hiowutura* (windbreak) around our dwelling. It was made of stalks bound together with a type of twine. I played in the space between the dwelling and the windbreak. This is how I learned to make a windbreak.

Fig. 11.2

Three types of cradle used by the Comanche are shown, l to r, ca. 1980: a *haabikuno;* a toy *waakohno* that belonged to Weckeah as a child; and a special beaded *turokohno*. L to r: Weckeah's sister, Nina Youngman; Weckeah; her nieces Mary Ann and Kay Youngman; her daughter Huwuni Bradley; Juanita Pahdopony; and Weckeah's granddaughter Susi Bradley, seated. Courtesy Weckeah Bradley Collection.

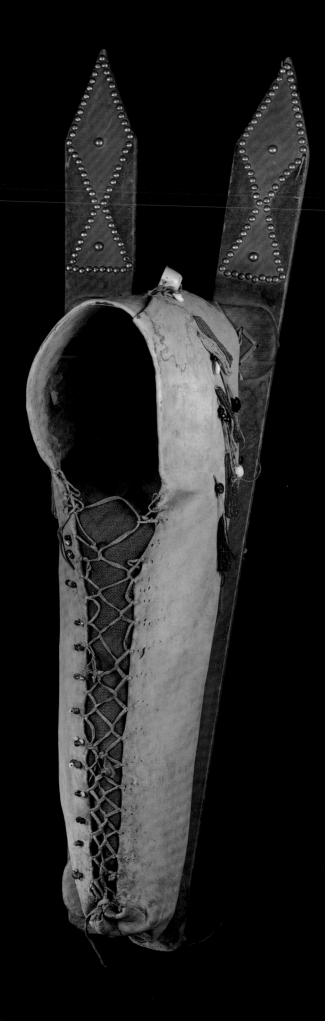

Fig. 11.3
Lattice cradle, Comanche, used by the
children of Quanah Parker. L: 118 cm.
Boards rubbed with red, green pigment,
silver tacks inserted; hide cover,
unbeaded, dyed with yellow pigment,
attachments of glass necklace beads,
shells, ceramic cup; no lining. Panhandle
Plains Historical Museum, Canyon,
Texas 3/77.

Fig. 11.4
Quanah and Weckeah Parker,
grandparents of Weckeah. Courtesy
Weckeah Bradley Collection.

Fig. 11.5
Putsi (Mary) Parker, mother of Weckeah. Courtesy Weckeah Bradley Collection.

In the winter when the hackberries were just right, my folks would gather them. Kaku prepared some goodies for me made of pounded hackberries rolled in just enough beef tallow to form them into large marshmallow-sized balls and put them in a container. They looked so pretty all flaked with red from the hackberry skins. They tasted so good when she toasted some for me on a peeled green limb held over the campfire.

Summertime we all moved out under the brush arbor. I remember sitting with my kaku on her *pisoona* (pallet) on the ground under the arbor. She would be doing beadwork using tiny seed beads. I still have some of the beaded things she gave me that she made. Her favorite colors were red, blue, and white. She gave me some buttons and a piece of twine to string them on so I would stay out of her beads. That was the beginning of my learning to bead. She had a nice ball of beeswax used for picking up tiny beads. It looked so inviting, reminding me of my hackberry goodies. One day I could not resist. I took a big bite out of the beeswax with red beads. There was a great commotion, but in the end everything was all right.

Fig. 11.6
Tupusiup (Alice) Parker, Weckeah's aunt, who made two doll cradles for her. Courtesy Weckeah Bradley Collection.

Drawings by Weckeah.

My doll cradle (waakohno) and doll with buckskin face and real hair.

My pia made me a little *waakohno* (cedar cradle) and a doll with a buckskin face and real hair. I would lace my doll up in the cradle and put the cradle strap around my chest and walk around with my doll cradle on my back. I still have that little cradle. Among my other toys were a family of finger-sized doll rags my pia made for me. They were dressed in Comanche cloth clothes. There was a mother, father, big brother, little sister and a baby in a *haabikuno* (night cradle). My brother and sister had a set of these dolls too, and we played with them together, pretending to go after wood in our wagons made of empty matchboxes. It wasn't effeminate for boys to have dolls. We even built mini bows and brush arbors. That's how my brother and I learned to make arbors.

My pia made a large doll cradle for me when I was older. My buckskin doll was a little small for that cradle. However, I had a little dog with a long tail named Kwasi (Tail), and she seemed just the right size for my new cradle. As I was placing her in the cradle, her tail must have gotten pinched and she began to cry. Pia told me to take Kwasi out because I was hurting her. After a while when my dog was calm, I figured out how

to put her in the cradle without hurting her tail. She was on her haunches with her front paws in the "sit up" position. I laced the cradle up as carefully as I could. Then I told her a baby story and sang her a lullaby. She went right to sleep. I thought her little pointed face looked so sweet peeping out from the doll cradle. She just fit it. That was the beginning of my telling our Comanche stories. Sometimes we received used toys from the missionaries. That's how I got a wooden, jointed doll. Because it had no hair my older sister painted black hair on its head. It fit my doll cradle perfectly and I forgot about putting Kwasi in the cradle.

When I was about seven years old, I remember my folks (usually my father) would put up a swing cradle made of rope and a blanket folded over several times going in and out – over and under the four (two on each side) lines of rope that were strung between two trees. Two sticks at least a foot long and about two inches in diameter were placed appropriately, separating the blanket at the head and foot. The baby's weight held the folded blanket securely in place. My sister and I were swinging the baby in just such a swing by pulling the attached rope. I had tied the rope to my foot so that my hands would be free to play. We were sitting on the ground tossing my mother's kickball to each other. I

Telling a story to a baby in a haabikuno (night cradle).

Sleeping in his baby swing (natsawenitʉ).

missed the ball and started going after it, forgetting about the rope attached to my foot and tripped myself. Fortunately I did not upset the swing cradle but I was much more cautious after that. Mother and Auntie made swings like that for my babies and, learning from them, I made them for my grandchildren. I was told that long ago tanned hide with hair left on was used instead of a blanket, and the rope was made from four or sometimes eight strands of braided buckskin. I plan to make a swing in this way, using an eight strand buckskin rope I have braided, and a soft deerskin with fur on the outside to hold the baby. The sticks, used to separate the skin at the head and foot, will be made of peeled soapberry limbs. It is a strong and lightweight wood. For the same reason I use this wood for my teepee staubs.

There are several types of Comanche cradles I have made for my grandchildren, a great-grandchild, and also for the baby of Elaine Miles of TV's Northern Exposure. The *waakohno* (cedar carrier) is an everyday cradle made of two cedar boards about three inches wide and about three feet, nine inches long with pointed tops. These long cedar boards go in the back with cross pieces at the head and foot. The material that actually

holds the baby is usually made of buckskin and sometimes canvas. The hood support, backing and footrest are made of firm rawhide. The loops and laces are made of narrow buckskin thongs. There is usually some decoration of either brass or silver head tack designs on the two boards showing above the hood on either side. The designs on the side are painted with red, green, or yellow powdered rock paint. The red rock paint is called "equipsia." Sometimes long strands of pony beads are draped over the hood and tied on each side resting lightly over the lower laced front. The strong leather carrying strap is attached to the outside of each of the boards about two inches down from the top cross piece, and goes across the mother's chest when she carries the cradle. I have seen and made long narrow strands of buckskin hanging gracefully down the back between the upright boards, also shorter fringes hanging from below at the foot of the cradle. The *tʉrokohno* or *tsomo waakohno* (beaded cradle) is made like the day cradle only it is completely decorated with beadwork (usually small seed beads). The beads are usually sewn directly onto the buckskin and cover the top, sides, and foot at

My grandmother carrying my mother in her beaded cradle (tʉrokohno or tsomo waakohno).

the bottom, also there is beadwork on a small rectangular buckskin piece to hide where the cross pieces are attached. The haabikʉno simply means "lying down holder." I have never seen or heard of this kind of cradle being carried on the back. It is made of rolled rawhide shaped in an oval shape on top. I have seen one cut straight across the top. The foot piece (almost square shaped) may be sewn at the bottom using an awl and sinew or it may be cut before the rawhide is rolled. The two slits are made on the bottom and on the sides at the foot where it is to be folded up and sewn in place using an awl and sinew. The holes for the loops start at the top where the baby's shoulders would be and go down to the foot and across the bottom of the foot and up the other side. The loops are made of a long narrow strip of buckskin going through each hole. Three narrow strips are cut for the lacing: two long and one shorter. The long strips are attached to the center loop, one above the other. The top strip is laced through the loops going upward. The lower one is laced going downward. The smaller strip is attached to the bottom loop and is laced going upward to meet the lower long strip. The two top ties are attached on each side to the top loops or there may be holes for them. The waakohno and the tʉrokono are laced up the same way.

Our folks long ago knew the usefulness of their baby cradles. My own experience with having babies in a cradle is that they are all-around handy. The baby is always part of the family, not tucked away in a crib or nursery. While in the cradle the top laces may be loosened down to the center so the baby's arms may be out to play. There is no getting up in the wee hours. My babies slept all night. It is handy for toilet training. When the baby awakes from a nap, the mother can take the baby out to go on the ground (if outside) or put a container under it. This way the baby becomes accustomed to being clean and always lets you know when it's time.

As I do these illustrations my thoughts are of my grandmother's beadwork designs. I have never seen mother's beaded baby cradle. I have only heard of it. I remember a very old cradle (waakohno) around our place. It was made by my grandmother Weckeah. Although it was not fully beaded, there were decorations of twelve strands of small glass pony beads draped over the hood and tied with buckskin thongs on the sides. The cedar boards were decorated with brass tack buttons making diamond and other shaped designs. Inside the design boards were painted with green powdered rock paint edged in red and yellow. The fabric was made of soft buckskin. There is a photograph of grandfather with Aunt Wanada (Wʉnʉrʉ) and others sitting under a brush arbor, when Aunt Wanada was about ten years old (fig. 11.7). I was told the waakohno in that picture was my mother's baby cradle. I still have the strand of beads from the cradle. They have been worn as a long necklace with the very old buckskin dress that was handed down to me. This dress Grandmother Weckeah made by tanning the skin herself from the deer that Grandfather Quanah shot with his bow and arrows.

Always before making a cradle or anything else there were prayers for thanks, for the new baby and for the material and for its gathering and use. I continue in this road as I was shown and feel that those who taught me are with me. It gives a pleasant balance to my life.

Fig. 11.7
Quanah Parker (center) with his young daughter Wanada and
others. The cradle leaning against the sapling was Weckeah's
mother's baby cradle. Courtesy Sam DeVenney Collection 3-4.

Carolyn Hunt Lujan, Kiowa, in 1916, in one of two cradles given to her by her grandmother Julia Given Hunt, one of the first Kiowa women to be educated at the Carlisle Indian School. Julia was the daughter of Satank, a chief of the Kiowa during the conflicts of the 1870s. The mountain lion wrapping indicates that the infant is descended from an honored warrior. Carolyn, with her sister Christina Hunt Simmons and other descendants of cradle makers and those who had cradles in their families, has contributed her knowledge and memories to this project. Julia Given Hunt was not herself a cradlemaker. When an especially loved child was to be honored, cradles were sometimes commissioned from specialists who were known for their ability to create this fine work. Carolyn was unaware of the location of this cradle until research for this project matched her photograph with the cradle. Courtesy Carolyn Hunt Lujan Collection.

Nostalgia

by CHRISTINA HUNT SIMMONS, KIOWA

THE ART AND CRAFT of cradle making in Kiowa culture is rarely practiced today. It is a thing of the past, a lost art on the brink of extinction. It would probably be safe for me to state that very few individuals have these heirlooms in their immediate possession.

This exhibit and book will help to establish the history of, distribute information about, and instill appreciation for what was once a truly crafted artifact of color-coordinated beadwork design on native-tanned hide that was also put to practical use.

Our changing mode of living and gradual acculturation contributed to phasing out this art form at about the end of the third decade of this century. Cradles are now historical subjects as far as the Kiowa go, but many are still in existence, owned by private collectors, or in large and well known museums. Sadly, they are not accessible to general tribal members, who cannot see

them to appreciate the art of the master Kiowa craft workers. This exhibit permits a large variety of lattice cradles to go on a journey, all together, from place to place, across the country. I commend the individuals who had the determination to locate the existing cradles. Much effort has gone into research, travel, and personal interviews.

Hopefully, people of all ages who never had the opportunity to actually see a cradle close at hand will take advantage of this once-in-a-life-time privilege. When we, as Kiowas, see these cradles, we can take pride in the artistry that once existed. It is even possible that the art can be revived.

Personally, it will fulfill a nostalgia, since I grew up in a home where an aged maternal grandmother, Atah, made doll cradles for her grandchildren. I was one of the grandchildren.

Lattice cradle, Kiowa, ca.1895, purchased by Julia Given for her granddaughter Carolyn Hunt (b. 1916). L: 117.5 plus fringe. Wood, brass, cotton; canvas cover, hide trim, glass seed bead designs in large, isolated, abstract leaf shapes, three on each side, separate geometric designs around head; sides symmetrical in design, differ in color; replacement lining. The Philbrook Museum of Art, Tulsa, Roberta Campbell Lawson Collection 1947.19.59.

We Often Wonder Where They Are

by JIMMY ARTERBERRY, COMANCHE

COMANCHE PEOPLE typically are not materialistic. Everything has a life span and everything has value but they don't really hang onto things. If someone liked something, you didn't tell them "no," you gave it to them.

There was a man from California who was passing through and he came to visit and my grandparents liked him. He was very nice and he came a few times. He would kind of visit and would have dinner with the family after church, and one time when he was here he said that he liked those cradleboards, and the kids were all grown, so my grandparents said, "well, you know, you can have them if you like."

And so they gave him the cradles. The last I heard was that he went back to California, and we've talked about it and you know, we often wonder where they are.

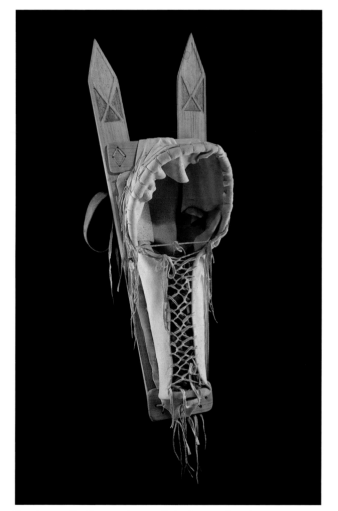

Lattice cradle, Comanche, made by Jimmy Arterberry, 1999. L: 112 cm. Cedar boards, painted, incised; brain-tanned and smoked elk cover, willow hood support, commercial leather carrying strap, rawhide backing, wooden footrest, elk tooth attachment. Haffenreffer Museum of Anthropology, Brown University 99-13-1. Photograph by Cathy Carver.

Wahperche, great-grandmother of Jimmy Arterberry, holding her baby, Flora Niyah Roach, in front of her face because she did not want her picture taken, 1904. Courtesy Jimmy Arterberry Collection.

They are gifts
of pride and love.

—SHARRON AHTONE HARJO

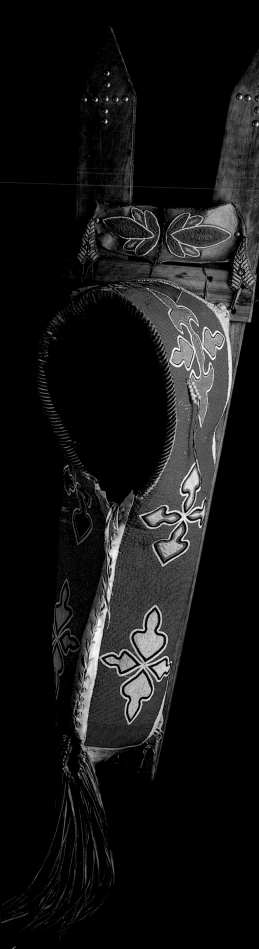

Tsomah (Mrs. George Poolaw) carrying granddaughter Linda Poolaw on her back in blanket. Courtesy Museum of the Great Plains, Sam DeVenney Collection 258.

Lattice cradle, Kiowa, made by Tsomah (Mrs. George Poolaw), ca. 1897, and used for all of her sons. L: 114 cm plus fringe. Wood, leather, canvas, cloth, glass beads, metal. Denver Art Museum, purchase from J. C. Tingley 1941.42.

Lattice cradle, Kiowa. In family of Dorothy Poolaw Ware, maker unknown. L: 115.5 cm plus fringe. Wood, tanned deerskin, canvas, cloth, glass seed beads, metal. Red Earth Museum, DeuPree Collection 87.5.18. Photograph by Jill Evans.

Justin Lee Ware, son of Dorothy Poolaw Ware, in Poolaw family cradle, Mountain View, Oklahoma, 1928. Courtesy Linda Poolaw and Stanford University. Photograph by Horace Poolaw.

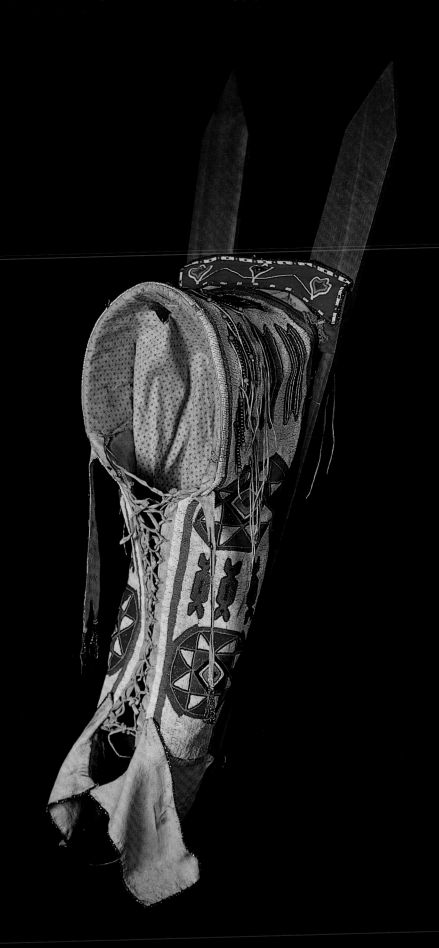

Lattice cradle, attributed to the Comanche, fully beaded in netted gourd stitch. L: 115.5 cm. Wood (bois d'arc), glass seed beads, necklace beads, brass tacks, muslin, cotton cloth, velvet, rawhide, commercial leather; bead design of small stylized leaf pattern, hexagons, connecting lines, color asymmetry in units of design. Denver Museum of Natural History, Crane American Indian Collection 11451. Photograph by Rick Wicker.

Nettie Odlety (Mrs. Parker McKenzie), Kiowa, with her nephew, Joe Guaddle in cradle, ca. 1920. Courtesy Western History Collections, University of Oklahoma Library, SWOC 122.

Lucille Permansu, Comanche, granddaughter of Codynah, ca. 1915, in family cradle possibly made by her grandmother or great-grandmother. Courtesy Sam DeVenney Collection 1-8.

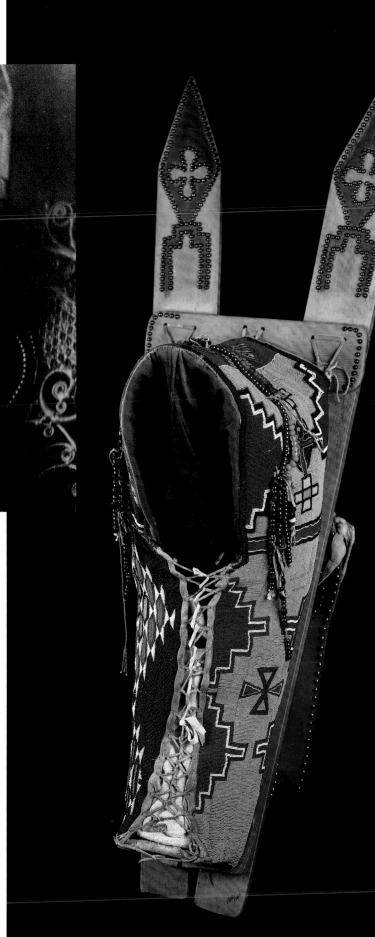

Lattice cradle, attributed to the Comanche, possibly made by Nahni, wife of medicine man Codynah (1868–1955), or by his mother. L: 114.5 cm. Boards painted red, green, outlined in tacks; cover fully beaded with sides asymmetric in color and design, a format favored by the Kiowa; footrest. Panhandle Plains Historical Museum, Canyon, Texas 1510/160.

Lattice cradle, Kiowa, ca. 1890. L: 111.5 cm plus fringe. Milled lumber, stained; rawhide: glass seed beads thread-sewn on canvas cover in Crow stitch and overlay stitch; tanned deerskin lacing and fringing. Fully beaded in geometric designs, symmetrical on each side but with different colors. Collected 1904. Fred Harvey Fine Arts Collection 83BE, The Heard Museum, Phoenix, Arizona.

Martha Napawat, Kiowa, with child in cradle. Martha was educated at the Carlisle Indian School in Pennsylvania. Her husband was Comanche. Courtesy Western History Collections, University of Oklahoma Library, Irwin Brothers Studio 9.

Lizzie Woodard, Kiowa, and child in cradle.
Courtesy Smithsonian Institution 42997c.

Lattice cradle and detail of other side, Kiowa,
used by Lizzie Woodard for her children
ca. 1890. L: 115.6 cm. Walnut frame, glass
beads, native tanned deerskin, rawhide, canvas,
calico. School of American Research M320.
Photographs reprinted, by permission, from
Legacy: Southwest Indian Art at the School
of American Research, Duane Anderson, ed.
Photographs by Addison Doty. ©1998, School
of American Research, Santa Fe.

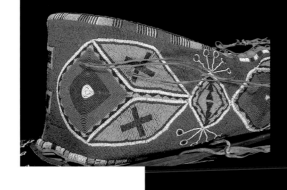

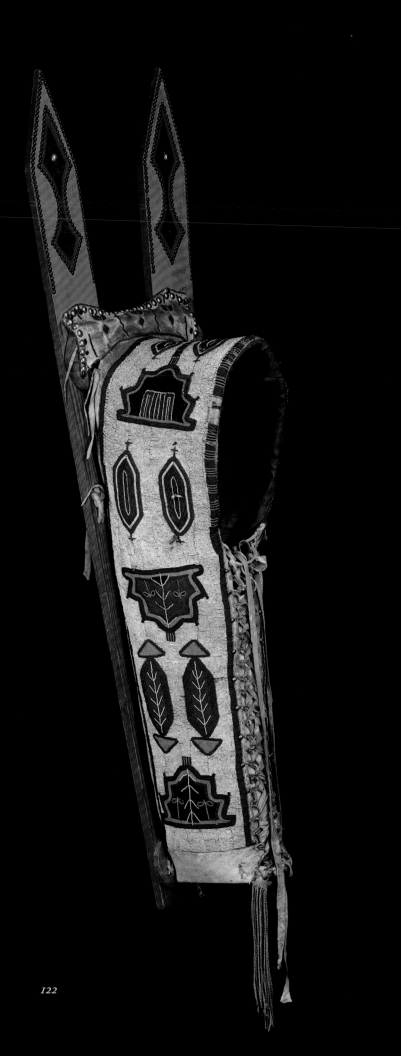

Lattice cradle, Kiowa, made by Doyetone c. 1904. L: 116 cm plus fringe. Milled lumber (pine), painted and decorated with white metal bosses, brass tacks; glass seed beads, sewn with cotton thread; tanned hide, canvas, cloth, wool; geometric and leaf-like figures beaded in contour and straight interior rows, and outlined in multiple (four to seven) rows; background in Crow stitch; sides of cover symmetrical in bead colors and design. Collected by George Gorton 1945, the cradle had long been in the possession of a single Kiowa family, whose name was hand-written in museum records as "Dogheto." No such name exists among the Kiowa, but Doyetone was the name of a well-known bead-worker. Margaret Bear, a grandchild, recognized Doyetone's particular leaf pattern in a photograph of this cradle and stated that there had been such a cradle in the family. The historic photograph of grandson Bill Bear in the cradle affirmed her belief that this was Doyetone's cradle. Milwaukee Public Museum E57416-18364.

William "Bill" Bear (b. 1904) eldest son of Amie Honemeeda and John Bert Bear, in cradle made by his maternal grandmother, Doyetone. Note that boards are different than those on cradle today. Courtesy Sam DeVenney Collection 1-11.

Amie Honemeeda Bear, (1876–1921) ca. 1890,
wearing cradle made by her mother Doyetone,
according to her granddaughters Dorothy White
Horse DeLaune and Joycetta Bear Elliott.
Courtesy Sam DeVenney Collection 1-14.

Lattice cradle, Kiowa, probably made by
Doyetone (1853–1926) about 1890, according to
her granddaughters Dorothy White Horse
DeLaune and Joycetta Bear Elliott. L: 109 cm
plus fringe. Boards painted, silver tacks; tanned
deerskin, canvas, glass beads in white, blues,
red, green, Crow and lazy stitch; multiple borders, no raised outlining; hide bib with leaf or
floral design; sides of cover symmetrical in colors and geometric designs of vertical striping,
diamonds; hide tabs forked, bead edged, yellow
dyed; carrying strap a red woven sash. The
Heard Museum, Phoenix, Fred Harvey Fine
Arts Collection 82BE.

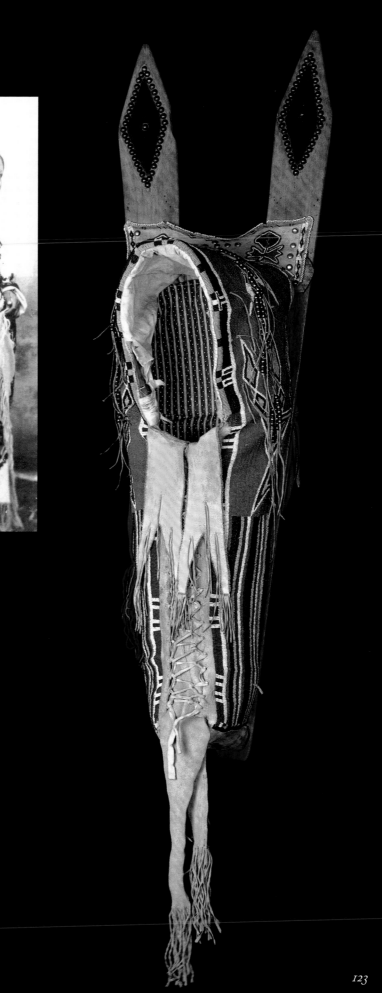

Boy from Carnegie with child in red wool cradle.
Other photographs show the cradle with cradle
maker Paukeigope and with Lois Smoky and her
baby. Courtesy Museum of the Great Plains, Sam
DeVenney 1059.

Lattice cradle, Kiowa, partially beaded on red
wool broadcloth, 1910–20. L: 111.5 cm plus fringe.
Wood, broadcloth, glass beads, brass studs, leather,
cotton cloth, silk ribbon. Leaf design, long, twisted
fringing, attachments of necklace beads and religious medal. Gilcrease Museum, Tulsa 8426.633.

Lattice cradle, Comanche, 1880–1900, used by Mary Buffalo. L: 109.5 cm. Wood, canvas, native tanned deerhide, rawhide, plain weave cotton, glass seed beads netted in flat gourd stitch, in small, geometric designs in red, blue, green, pink, yellow on white background; sides of cover symmetrical in design, differ in colors. German silver buttons. Very few netted cradles exist, most attributed to the Comanche. Collected by Mark Raymond Harrington, 1916, for the National Museum of the American Indian, Smithsonian Institution 5/7467. Photograph by Cathy Carver.

Mary Buffalo *(Ygetop)*, Kiowa, ca. 1916, carrying cradle on horseback, next to the Tipi with Battle Pictures, which belonged to her husband Oheltoint, a descendant of the Kiowa leader Tohausen II. Oheltoint was the brother of the artist Silver Horn and of cradle-maker Keintaddle. The photograph is posed, one of several taken at a public gathering about 1916; another photograph shows a sign inviting the public into the tipi for a small entrance fee, and her appearance on horseback with the cradle is undoubtedly part of the attraction. Mary Buffalo's first husband was Comanche, and the cradle may have been a gift to their son. Courtesy Western History Collections, University of Oklahoma Library, Phillips 725.

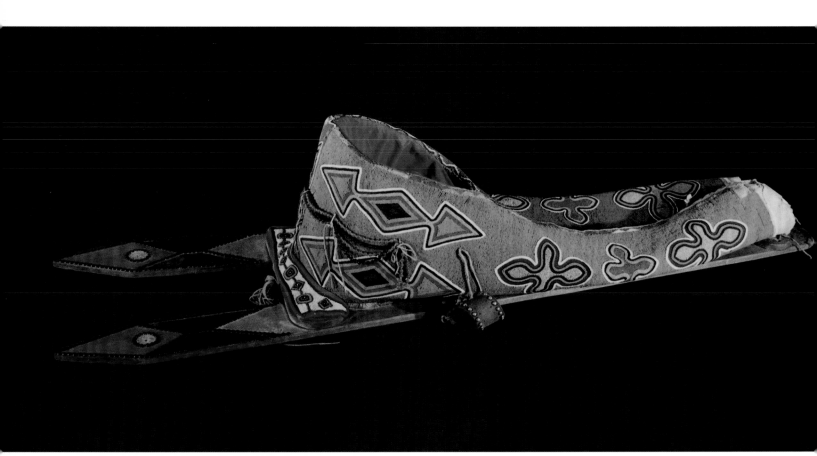

Lattice cradle, Kiowa cover, Comanche boards, 1890–1900.
L: 120.5 cm; glass beads, hide, cloth, wood, brass brads; bead
designs large, separated, curvilinear and geometric shapes, sewn
on canvas in Crow and overlay stitch, with raised outlining,
background color green on one side, blue on other; bib. Green
and yellow painted boards in Comanche style have replaced the
earlier unpainted Kiowa style boards in photograph of Lois
Smoky (see frontispiece). Purchased by trader Arthur Lawrence
from the Comanche Monetathchi family in 1925. Museum of
the Great Plains, Lawton, Oklahoma 86.14.48. Photograph by
Alexandra O'Donnell.

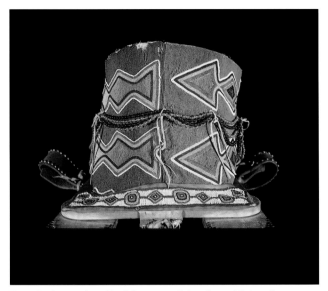

Detail of top of cradle. Museum of the Great Plains, Lawton,
Oklahoma 86.14.48. Photograph by Brian Smith.

Lattice cradle, Kiowa, made by sisters Sau'totauto
and Autoinonah for the baby of Autoinonah's
daughter, Helen Koomsa, ca. 1899. Each sister
beaded one side. L: 100 cm plus fringe. Wood,
rawhide, glass seed beads thread-sewn directly on
native tanned deerskin, in lazy stitch, Crow stitch,
overlay stitch; canvas and cotton linings, necklace
beads, velvet bib; deerskin wraps over top horizontal slat and ties in back in early style, and natural
shape of deerskin used to form tabs and fringing.
Bead designs, slightly different on each side, of
delicate hook and line extensions evoke Caucasian
carpet designs. Late 19th century Southwest
traders distributed similar patterns to Navajo
weavers. Collected by Col. Edward L. Wilcox,
1901, in Mountain View, Oklahoma. Field Museum
of Natural History, Chicago 205285, neg. A113863c.
Photo by John Weinstein.

Sau'totauto (Mrs. White Buffalo) and Autoinonah
(Mrs. Eunap), 1929. They were the daughters
of the Kiowa chief Satanta. Courtesy Georgia
DuPoint Collection.

Alma Big Tree Ahote (standing) and sister Marietta, daughters of Chief Big Tree, ca. 1893. Courtesy Western History Collections, University of Oklahoma Library, Campbell 191.

Toy cradles made by Alma Big Tree Ahote (1884–1964) for her great-nieces in 1955. Green cradle with cloth doll, L: 37 cm, Marguerite Tsoodle Lee Collection. Blue cradle with bib, L: 30 cm, Sharon Toyebo Hunter Collection. Photograph by Sandy Settle.

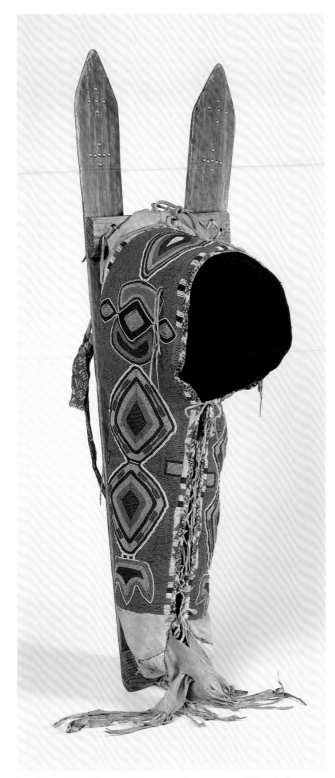

Model lattice cradle, Kiowa, made by Richard Aitson, Kiowa/Kiowa-Apache, 1999. L: 57 cm. Fully beaded using white-core rose and other early beads. Elements Beadery Collection, Bethany, Oklahoma. Photograph by Richard Aitson.

Lattice cradle, Kiowa, 1880–1900. L: 100.4 cm. Wood, German silver tacks, native tanned deerskin cover fully beaded in abstract designs with multiple outlining; hide edging and fringe; woolen and cotton cloth. Fenimore Art Museum, Cooperstown, New York, Thaw Collection T77. Photograph by John Bigelow Taylor.

Infant Tennis Shoes, made by Teri Greeves, Kiowa/Comanche, 1997. L: 13 cm. The bead images are inspired by ledger art. Haffenreffer Museum of Anthropology, Brown University 97-9.

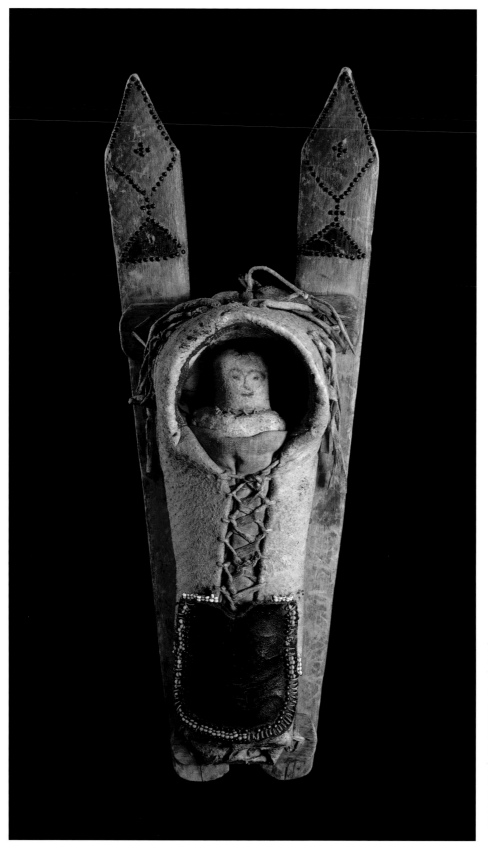

Toy cradle with hide doll, Comanche, ca. 1895. L: 32.5 cm. Wood, native tanned hide, commercial leather, glass seed beads, pigments, silk. Although a toy, it has all the characteristics of a full-size cradle (waakohno) for a boy, with bead-edged si'wuparru, wooden footrest, painted and tack-decorated boards. The hide doll has a painted face and human hair. Private collection. Photogaph by Cathy Carver.

Contributors

SHEPARD KRECH III is Director of the Haffenreffer Museum of Anthropology and Professor of Anthropology, Brown University. His research interests include North American ethnology, ethnohistory, and museology. He is co-editor of *Collecting Native America, 1870–1960*, Smithsonian Institution Press, 1999. His most recent book is *The Ecological Indian, Myth and History*, Norton, N.Y., 1999.

N. SCOTT MOMADAY is a Kiowa Pulitzer prize-winning author as well as an artist and story-teller, and is the descendant of known bead artists (see his book *The Names*). As a child he spent much time with his grandparents in the Kiowa community of Mountain View, about which he wrote in *The Way to Rainy Mountain*. Their home was just across the road from the home of cradle maker Millie Durgan Goombi (Saintohoodle). Momaday is a Professor of English at the University of Arizona.

BARBARA A. HAIL is Deputy Director and Curator of the Haffenreffer Museum of Anthropology, Brown University. Her research interests include North American Plains and Subarctic ethnology and ethnohistory. She is the author of two books that discuss stylistic and cultural aspects of the material culture of these areas: *Hau, Kola!* (Plains) and [with Kate Duncan] *Out of the North* (Subarctic). Recent research has included the history of museums. She is co-editor of *Collecting Native America, 1870–1960*, Smithsonian Institution Press, 1999. Since 1995 she has been investigating the cultural significance of Kiowa and Comanche cradles with descendants of cradle makers and current cradle makers.

EVERETT R. RHOADES of Oklahoma City, Oklahoma, is a Kiowa physician who in 1982 became the first Indian director of the Indian Health Service. He was selected Outstanding Indian of the Year at the American Indian Exposition in 1996. He is presently Adjunct Professor in International Health at Johns Hopkins University and an Associate Dean at the University of Oklahoma College of Medicine. He is of both Kiowa and non-Indian descent, as a grandson of Dr. James and Maud (Tahote) Rowell through whose family three Kiowa cradles came to the Haffenreffer Museum of Anthropology.

BEATRICE AHPEAHTONE DOYAH SMITH, Kiowa, of Anadarko, Oklahoma, owns a cradle made by her grandmother Guohaddle, a wife of Chief Ahpeahtone, last federally recognized chief of the Kiowa people. As a child she observed her grandmother at work on beaded articles and noted how she made her design motifs. She has numerous family photographs showing cradle use, and is familiar with stories of her own and other families' cradles. She has loaned her cradle to the exhibition.

RAY DOYAH, of Anadarko, Oklahoma, great-grandson of Kiowa cradle maker Guohaddle, is a writer and poet. He has prepared an illustrated family genealogy for the exhibition with photographs of Guohaddle's descendants over the past 88 years who have been pictured in the cradle she made.

JUANITA PAHDOPONY-MITHLO, of Lawton, Oklahoma, is a Comanche artist and educator, and Tribal Administrator for the Comanche Tribal Council. She and her father, Sam Pahdopony, have loaned their family cradle to the exhibition. She has represented this cradle, or designs from it, on a number of her art pieces.

BERNADINE HERWONA TOYEBO RHOADES of Oklahoma City is the Kiowa granddaughter and great-granddaughter respectively of cradle makers Atah and Keintaddle, and has contributed a chapter on each of them to this publication.

SHARRON AHTONE HARJO, is a Kiowa tribal member, and an art instructor, painter and basket maker living in Oklahoma City, Oklahoma. Her paintings are in the collections of the Oklahoma Historical Society; Haffenreffer Museum of Anthropology; Southern Plains Indian Museum; Center for Great Plains Studies, Univ. of Nebraska, Lincoln; and she has exhibited at numerous institutions. Her paintings of Saynday, the Kiowa trickster-hero, and of the sun dance, traveled with the 1997 S.I.T.E.S. exhibit "Saynday was coming along…Silverhorn's Drawings of the Kiowa Trickster." She has won the Outstanding Indian Woman of Oklahoma Award from the Oklahoma Federation of Indian Women; was Miss Indian America in 1966; and has served on the Board of Directors of the Southern Plains Indian Museum and the annual Red Earth festival, Oklahoma City. Sharron is the granddaughter of cradle maker Tahdo and the great-granddaughter of cradle maker Millie Durgan (Saintohoodle). She has loaned her family cradles to this exhibition, and has shared in all phases of its planning.

JACOB AHTONE, of Anadarko, Oklahoma, is a Kiowa elder, former tribal chairman, and chairman of the board of the Kiowa Tribal Museum. He is the son of cradle maker Tahdo and the grandson-in-law of cradle maker Millie Durgan (Saintohoodle). He watched his mother create bead designs, and his father make the hand-hewn lattice framework for cradles. He has served as a primary consultant among Kiowa elders in the Anadarko region, and as on-site coordinator for the oral history project on video and audio tape.

VANESSA PAUKEIGOPE JENNINGS, of Fort Cobb, Oklahoma, is a Kiowa beadworker who has dedicated her life to continuing the artistic traditions she learned as a child from her grandmother, who was a distinguished artist of her own generation. Paukeigope is descended from prominent artists on both sides of her family (artist Stephen Mopope, and beadworkers/ cradle makers Jeanette Berry Mopope, Paukeigope (Etta) Mopope, Keintaddle, and Anna Jones Berry). In both 1989 and 1990 Paukeigope was awarded a National Heritage Fellowship from the National Endowment for the Arts. She has demonstrated her art in numerous European nations. At the 1996 Plains Indian Art Conference in Cody, Wyoming she and her work were honored as the subject of the key-note address. Paukeigope has made two dozen full-size cradles in the past ten years. One of these is in the current exhibition.

WECKEAH BRADLEY, of Lawton, Oklahoma, is a Comanche cradle maker and artist who has made a haabikʉno or night cradle for this exhibition. The pencil drawings in her chapter are her own. She is the granddaughter of Quanah Parker and his first wife Weckeah. She served in the U.S. Marine Corps during World War II.

CHRISTINA HUNT SIMMONS, of Mountain View, Oklahoma, is a Kiowa elder, a great-granddaughter of the famed Kiowa chief Satank (Set-ankeah, Setank, Sitting Bear) and a granddaughter of cradle maker Atah, whose cradle she has loaned to this exhibition.

JIMMY ARTERBERRY of Medicine Park, Oklahoma, is a Comanche artist and cradle maker, descended from a number of cradle makers, one of whom taught him the skill. He has made a "try-on" Comanche cradle for this exhibition.

Bibliography

Annual Report of the Board of Regents of the Smithsonian Institution. National Museum Report for 1887, and Report of the United States National Museum for the year ending June 30, 1894. Washington: Government Printing Office

Appadurai, Arjun 1986
The Social Life of Things. Cambridge University Press. Cambridge.

Berlandier, Jean Louis 1969
The Indians of Texas in 1830. Edited and introduction by John C. Ewers. Smithsonian Institution Press, Washington, D.C.

Berlo, Janet, ed. 1996
Plains Indian Drawings, 1865–1935. Abrams, New York.

Boyd, Maurice 1981
Kiowa Voices: Ceremonial Dance, Ritual and Song. Vol. I. Linn Pauahty, Kiowa Consultant. Kiowa Historical and Research Society, Consultants. Texas Christian University Press, Fort Worth.

Boyd, Maurice 1983
Kiowa Voices: Myths, Legends and Folktales. Vol. II. Linn Pauahty, Chairman, Kiowa Historical and Research Society. Helen McCorpin and Jane Pattie, assoc. eds., The Susan Peters Collection. Texas Christian University Press, Fort Worth.

Campos, Rosemary Gates 1989
"Soothing Pain-elicited Distress in Infants with Swaddling and Pacifiers." In Lipsitt and Reese, pp. 81–792.

Catlin, George 1973 [1844]
Letters and Notes on the Manners, Customs, and Conditions of North American Indians. Vol. II. Dover Publications, New York. Reprint.

Chisholm, James 1983
"The Cradleboard." In *Navajo Infancy: An Ethological Study of Child Development,* pp. 71–92. Aldine Publishing Co., New York.

De Mause, Lloyd, ed. 1995
The History of Childhood. Jacob Aronson, Inc., Northvale, New Jersey, London.

Feder, Norman 1965
American Indian Art. Abrams, New York.

Foster, Michael R. 1996
"Language and the Culture History of North America." In Goddard ed., pp. 64–110.

Foster, Morris W. 1991
Being Comanche: A Social History of an American Indian Community. University of Arizona press, Tucson.

Ghibely, A. 1990
"La maladie luxante chez les Indiens du Quebec." In *Acta Orthopaedica Belgica,* vol. 56, 1, pp. 37–42.

Goddard, Ives 1996
"The Classification of the Native Languages of North America." In Goddard ed., pp. 290–323.

Goddard, Ives, ed. 1996
Language. *Handbook of North American Indians, vol. 17.* Smithsonian Institution, Washington, DC.

Gorer, Geoffrey 1962
"Development of the Swaddling Hypothesis." In *The People of Great Russia: A Psychological Study,* pp. 197–226. Norton, New York.

Greene, Candace 1992
Soft Cradles of the Central Plains. *Plains Anthropologist,* Journal of the Plains Anthropological Society. Vol. 37: 95–113.

Greene, Candace
In Press. *Silver Horn: Master Illustrator of the Kiowa.* University of Oklahoma Press, Norman.

Hail, Barbara A. 1983
Hau, Kola! The Plains Indian Collection of the Haffenreffer Museum of Anthropology. Brown University, Bristol, Rhode Island.

Hail, Barbara A. 1994
"The Ethnographic Collection." in *Passionate Hobby: Rudolf Frederick Haffenreffer and the King Philip Museum,* pp. 91–134. Shepard Krech III, ed. Brown University, Bristol, Rhode Island.

Harper's Weekly. 1867 6(543):329 (May 25, 1867). New York, N.Y.

Hays, Joe S. 1995
"The Arthur R. Lawrence Collection in the Museum of the Great Plains, pp. 38–49, *American Indian Art Magazine,* Spring.

Hudson, Charles 1966
"Isometric Advantages of the Cradle Board: A Hypothesis." *American Anthropologist* (68): 470–474.

Jacknis, Ira 1999
"Patrons, Potters, and Painters: Phoebe Hearst's Collections from the American Southwest." In *Collecting Native America, 1870–1960,* pp. 139–171. Shepard Krech III and Barbara A. Hail, eds. Smithsonian Institution Press, Washington and London.

James, Edwin 1966
Account of an Expedition from Pittsburgh to the Rocky Mountains. 2 vols. Ann Arbor, MI, University Microfilms.

Kavanaugh, Thomas W. 1995
"Comanche and Kiowa Cradles in Historical Photographs." Paper presented at the Native American Art Studies Association Conference, Tulsa, Oklahoma.

Kincaide, Reese 1939
Genuine Indian Bead Work and Art Goods: The Mohonk Lodge, Colony, Oklahoma. Clinton, Oklahoma.

Krech, Shepard, III 1994
    "Introduction." In *Passionate Hobby: Rudolf Frederick Haffenreffer and the King Philip Museum,* pp. 9–16. Shepard Krech III, ed. Brown University, Bristol, Rhode Island.

Krech, Shepard, III, and Barbara A. Hail, eds. 1999
    Collecting Native America, 1870–1960. Smithsonian Institution Press, Washington and London.

LaBarre, Weston, William Bascom, Donald Collier, Bernard Mishkin and Jane Richardson 1935
    Papers of Weston LaBarre, *Notes on Kiowa Ethnography, Santa Fe Laboratory of Anthropology Expedition.* Smithsonian Institution, Washington, D.C.

Lipsitt, Lewis P. and Hayne W. Reese 1979
    Child Development. Scott, Foresman and Company, Glenview, Illinois

Lipton, Earle L., Alfred Steinschneider, and Julius B. Richmond 1965 "Swaddling, a Child Care Practice: Historical Cultural and Experimental Observations," *Pediatrics,* Supplement, 35, part 2 (March): 521–67.

Marriott, Alice 1945
    The Ten Grandmothers. The Civilization of the American Indian Series. University of Oklahoma Press, Norman.

Marriott, Alice 1967
    Kiowa Years. A Study in Culture Impact. Macmillan Company, New York, Collier-MacMillan Limited, London.

Mason, Otis T. 1912
    "Cradles." In *Handbook of American Indians North of Mexico.* Bureau of American Ethnology Bulletin No. 30, Part 1, pp. 357–359. F. W. Hodge, ed. Government Printing Office, Washington, D.C.

Mayhall, Mildred P. 1971
    The Kiowas. The Civilization of the American Indian Series, vol. 63. University of Oklahoma Press, Norman.

Merrill, William, Marian Kaulity Hansson, Candace Greene, and Frederick Reuss 1996 "A Guide to the Kiowa Collections at the Smithsonian Institution." *Contributions to Anthropology No. 40,* Smithsonian Institution Press.

Mishkin, Bernard 1940
    Rank and Warfare among the Plains Indians. University of Washington Press, Seattle.

Mollhausen (Heinrich) Baldwin 1858
    Diary of a Journey from the Mississippi to the Coasts of the Pacific with a United States Government Expedition. Vols. I, II. Introduction by Alexander Von Humboldt and illustrations in chromo-lithography; translated by Mrs. Percy Sinnett. Longman, Brown, Green, Longmans and Roberts, London.

Momaday, N. Scott 1989
    The Names. Doubleday, New York.

Mooney, James 1979
    (reprint) with Introduction by John C. Ewers from 1896 Calendar History of the Kiowa Indians. *Annual Report, Bureau of American Ethnology* 17 (1).

Newcomb, William W. 1961
    The Indians of Texas from Prehistoric to Modern Times. University of Texas Press, Austin.

Newcomb, William W. 1978
    German Artist of the Texas Frontier, Friedrich Richard Petri. University of Texas Press, Austin.

Nye, Wilbur Sturtevant 1962
    Bad Medicine and Good. University of Oklahoma Press, Norman.

Nye, Wilbur Sturtevant 1968a
    (reprint) *Carbine and Lance: The Story of Old Fort Sill.* University of Oklahoma Press, Norman.

Nye, Wilbur Sturtevant 1968b
    (reprint) *Plains Indian Raiders: The Final Phases of Warfare from the Arkansas to the Red River, with Original Photographs by William S. Soule.* University of Oklahoma Press, Norman.

Petersen, Karen Daniels 1968
    Plains Indian Art from Fort Marian. University of Oklahoma Press, Norman.

Reese, Hayne W. and Lewis P. Lipsitt 1970
    Experimental Child Psychology. Scott, Foresman and Co., Glenview, Illinois.

Schneider, Mary Jane 1982
    "Connections: Family Ties in Kiowa Art." In *Pathways to Plains Prehistory: Anthropological Perspectives of Plains Natives and their Pasts,* pp. 7–18. Don G. Wyckoff and Jack L. Hoffman, eds. *Oklahoma Anthropological Society Memoir No. 3,* The Cross Timbers Heritage Association. Norman, Oklahoma.

Schneider, Mary Jane 1983
    "Kiowa and Comanche Baby Carriers." *Plains Anthropologist,* Journal of the Plains Anthropological Society. Vol. 28 (1): 305–314.

Tronick, E. Z. and R. B. Thomas and M. Baltabuit 1994
    "The Quechua Manta Pouch: A Caretaking Practice for Buffering the Peruvian Infant against the Multiple Stressors of High Altitude." In Lipsitt and Reese, pp. 1005–1013.

Wallace, Ernest and E. Adamson Hoebel 1952
    The Comanches, Lords of the South Plains. University of Oklahoma Press, Norman.

Wright, Muriel H. 1986
    A Guide to the Indian Tribes of Oklahoma. University of Oklahoma Press, Norman and London.